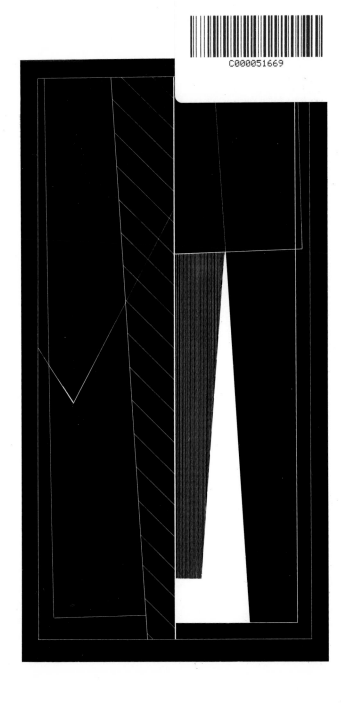

SAGE EYE

The Aesthetic Passion of Jonathan Griffin

a celebration in poetry and prose
edited by Anthony Rudolf

THE MENARD PRESS/KING'S COLLEGE
LONDON 1992

SAGE EYE:
THE AESTHETIC PASSION OF JONATHAN GRIFFIN

Cover design by Merlin James

Frontispiece made specially for this book by Julia Farrer

Photograph by John Vere Brown

Distribution in North America by
SPD Inc
1814 San Pablo Avenue
Berkeley, CA 94702, USA

ISBN 0 9513753 9 3

THE MENARD PRESS
8 The Oaks
Woodside Avenue
London N12 8AR
081-446-5571

KING'S COLLEGE LONDON
Adam Archive Publications
The Strand, London WC2R 2LS

Set and printed by Printhaüs Book Co. Ltd., Northampton

to Jonathan Griffin
and
for Kathleen Griffin
with love

ACKNOWLEDGMENTS

This book could not have been edited without the help and support of Kathleen Griffin whose good humour and common sense have guided her through the intricacies of such institutions as marriage, church, theatre and small press publishing. The male ego looms large in these environments. It is a magnificent edifice but extremely fragile. Because she has always understood this, because even after a tiring day she can do three things at once (knit, stroke the cat and read books), because she is so funny and because she has no side (as Jonathan would have said), we honour her, a glorious Englishwoman and the most generous friend in the world.

CONTENTS

Anthony Rudolf (introduction) 6
Jonathan Griffin (letter) 14
Rachel Blau DuPlessis (poem) . . _ 17
Keith Bosley (poem) 18
Tom Courtenay 22
Jonathan Delamont 23
Christopher Fry 26
The Revd. John Gilling 27
Giles Gordon 29
John Greenhalgh 36
Ronald Harwood 38
Peter Hiley 40
Roland Hill 42
The Revd. Dr. Brian Horne 44
Bernard and Jane Horsfall 46
Peter Hoy/René Char (poem & commentary) . . 47
The Revd. Frederick Jackson SSC 49
Ivan Jelinek 51
Louis and Annette Kaufman 56
Sir John Lawrence 58
Karin Lessing (poem) 63
Eugenio Lisboa 64
Helder Macedo 65
Jeremy Noble 68
Paul Oppenheimer 71
P.K. Paige (poem) 72
David Pinner (poem) 73
Lawrence Pitkethly 75
Neville Price 80
Kathleen Raine 82
Carl Rakosi (poem) 85
Manuel Rosenthal 86
Dee September (poem) 87
Sebastian Shaw (& Joan Ingpen-Shaw) 88
Matthew Sweeney (poem) 90
Frank Thornton 91
Judith Thurman 93
Daniel Weissbort 94
Susannah York 97
Bibliography 101
Contributors 102

INTRODUCTION
ANTHONY RUDOLF

I met Jonathan Griffin on December 31 1967 or January 1 1968, at Philippe Grandville's New Year's Eve party in the Lord's Gallery. When introduced to him by Annette Lavers I asked him if he was the same Jonathan Griffin who had translated Montherlant's *Le Maître de Santiago*. Yes. I told him he'd helped me survive my 'A' level French course some eight years earlier: his translation – found in North Finchley library's reserve stacks – had served as a crib. Not long after that began the close personal and professional association which continues to this day, since I am not only his publisher but also his literary executor. His very first Pessoa translation appeared in the *Griffin* issue of *The Journals of Pierre Menard*, the forerunner of *The Menard Press*.

Jonathan was both too modest and too busy with his main concerns to write an autobiography – and it is now too late for the tape-recorded interviews some of us had suggested. I used to tease him that the perfect title would be *A Margin for Greed*, a phrase which was part of his reply to my question about how he managed to keep so thin and fit given his regime – austere it was not. His insatiable and enchanting appetite for the arts is one of the defining characteristics of the man as traced through the contributions to this book, along with the gift of friendship and the high mastery of poetry and translation.

The book has gaps in two respects. Firstly, not everybody who was invited managed to contribute a piece. Secondly, not everything in his life has been covered. While not a hagiography, it does not even pretend to be a collective biography or critical portrait. It is a celebration. Jonathan Griffin, being human, was no saint, but he was a deeply loved man for reasons which come up time and again. Eventually, I believe, the tributes will interest people beyond his circle of friends, acquaintances, colleagues and admirers, but people out there must first discover his work. This is the right and proper way round, as Jonathan himself would have been the first to agree.

The poet and translator Jonathan Griffin was a man of the highest culture, a legend even among his circle of cultivated friends – who were drawn from all the arts (especially literature and music), the church, the universities and Fleet Street, and across all the generations, not to mention gender preferences. In his heyday the dinner parties cooked by his second wife Kate – a stylish, learned and shrewd woman whose combination of earthly commonsense, earthy humour and high church devotion complemented rather than reinforced Griffin's soft-spoken upper class reserve, retiring nature, gentle spirit and god-intoxicated agnosticism – were privileged round tables of talent off duty, occasionally genius, where new friendships were made and people felt they were companions of honour. Even the house cats were cats' cats. The house in Primrose Hill was a joy to visit (and still is...), with its heirloom paintings, leather bound books, Sweet Afton fags, malt whisky galore and good fellowship. Aldeburgh, where the Griffins had a flat, was the home from home. Griffin was a familiar face at rehearsals, well respected by "Ben and Peter".

Young poets, painters and musicians, along with the cats, treated Jonathan as an honorary uncle, the lavish dispenser of wine (milk); he was normal enough to enjoy juicy gossip about love affairs and literary politics: these categories often overlapped of course, while the cats preened themselves on being above that sort of thing; more seriously, he was a mentor and enthusiast – as the biographer and novelist, his protégée, Judith Thurman wrote on his eightieth birthday: "When you listen to a piece of music with him, or walk along a path you thought familiar, or when he takes you into an old church, or reads to you from a new book, you become aware that his capacity for attentiveness – passion, fury, humility and precision – has grown stronger with the years, not weaker".

Jonathan Griffin was not a man you went to for heavy duty criticism when that was needed for a poem or translation or essay, for he would too readily give you the benefit of the doubt, suffer foolishness gladly. Perhaps he thought he would be risking pain or embarrassment in a friend. This benign fault, if fault it was, derived from the breadth of his generosity, the catholicity of his taste, the manifold circle of his enthusiasms. He was at his best *praising*, with rare lucidity and discernment, what he *loved* best. That was the gist of his serious conversation pieces, his rare incursions into reviewing and criticism, as well as being the matrix of his rigorous approach to the loved poetry he translated.

"He had the aesthetic passion to a degree that I have rarely encountered", wrote the actor Robert Speaight in his autobiography. Nor was Griffin a man who found it easy to speak his mind directly concerning his deepest feelings on personal matters, except where these coincided with green politics, the major concern of his last years and the backdrop to his poetry years before the theme became fashionable. He was a man of iron determination and generally got what he wanted, which was to enjoy himself doing congenial work – and he worked extremely hard – and then to enjoy himself in congenial play. Living a full life of sensations and thoughts, he never ceased courting the muse. His wife and other intimates would occasionally grumble, occasionally throw a wobbler, but it all worked out OK because the positive side so strongly outweighed the negative.

Griffin adored the company of women, not least the actresses he courted (two-timing the muse?) between his two marriages, often with red hair and Russian names. In later years Julia Farrer, the brilliant young painter who illustrated his books (and has contributed the frontispiece to this volume) and whose love and devotion should be placed on record, would escort the frail *melomane* to the modern music concerts less enjoyed by his wife.

Jonathan Griffin was born in Worthing in 1906. He had a traditional landed gentry upbringing in a military family, against whose conventions he rebelled early. Through his maternal grandfather he was a direct descendant of Edward Thurlow (1732–1806), Lord Chancellor of England. He was also a direct descendant of Louis Napoleon, whose illegitimate daughter married the same grandfather. He was educated at Radley School and New College

Oxford where he was an exact contemporary and acquaintance of Hugh Gaitskell, and a close associate of John Lawrence and Robert Speaight, who became lifelong friends. His first passion was music. He was almost good enough to be a pupil of Schnabel and only when he realised he would not reach those exalted heights did he abandon hopes of a career as a concert pianist. He was an intimate of the Dolmetsch family, who made a harpsichord for him. He gave the first ever (private) performance of Berg's piano sonata. Composers and performers of the stature of Boulez sought his approbation.

In the early thirties he married his first wife. He would henceforth see his future in terms of the word: journalism and writing books. At this time he was involved in anti-fascist organisations such as For Intellectual Liberty, alongside colleagues like V.S. Pritchett, Kingsley Martin, Henry Moore and Margaret Gardiner. He wrote a number of books on political and military matters, including *Britain's Air Policy* for Victor Gollancz, *Lost Liberty? The Ordeal of the Czechs*, and *Glass Houses in Modern War*. In 1939 he became the South-East Europe correspondent of the New York *Nation* and was based in Prague, where, characteristically, he met Tristan Tzara. His views on defence were adopted by the Liberal Party.

For most of the war Griffin was Director of BBC European Intelligence at Bush House, where he headed an unruly bunch of talented natives and refugees – including Miron Grindea the editor of *Adam*. The department's job was to sift reports from continental occupied Europe and supply background to the newsroom, with whom there was creative tension. At least some of his time was spent dealing with BBC intrigues from within, which experience was to colour his view of politics later on.

After the war he was appointed second secretary at the British embassy in Paris where he was, in effect and by design, cultural attaché: a description not in common use until years later. Paris after the liberation. The right place, the right time, the right man, and living in rue Notre Dame des Champs, the atmosphere memorably dunked in Speaight's autobiography. His friends included Jean-Louis Barrault, whose memoirs he later translated and Nadia Boulanger. Among the many people he brought over – in

9

the interests of Anglo-French understanding – was Bertrand Russell. He was in contact with many prominent writers, musicians and painters. He met Picasso in his studio, rue des Grands-Augustins, the one described by Balzac in *The Unknown Masterpiece*. Once, left alone in Braque's studio, he admired the patina on the painter's bronzes. When Braque returned Griffin asked him how he had achieved the effect: "Eh bien, je les ensevelis dans le jardin, et je pisse bien dessus".

On another occasion Jonathan was in the flat of Samuel Beckett (whose life span was one week shorter than Jonathan's) when the intercom buzzed. Beckett picked up the phone and grimaced at the name of an unwanted visitor (we must assume this was not Michael Horovitz who remembers something similar when calling up from the street on one of his visits). Winking at Griffin and affecting the gait and high-pitched voice of a lady's maid, Beckett said: "Je vais voir s'il est là". Beckett then tripped and minced his way round the table and, returning to the phone, announced: "Non, monsieur n'est pas là".

Privately Griffin supported the Attlee government, and in this he was typical of the more enlightened members of his class: noblesse oblige, common sense, decency. And even though in later years he became disillusioned with some Labour policies – occasioning polite but serious differences on defence with one obsessed younger friend – he never wavered in his view that the 1945–51 Labour government was the best and most efficient of the century.

The fifties saw him working on a number of translations to earn a living – Giono, Kazantzakis, Gary, de Gaulle's memoirs, art history books. But his deep reason for retiring from the diplomatic service was to work on a verse play of his own, a trilogy called *The Hidden King*, influenced by Fry, Eliot and Claudel, but in many respects original. About Sebastian of Portugal, it was published in 1955 and play-read at Cambridge, Massachusetts, under the auspices of Archibald MacLeish and Bill Alfred. Robert Lowell too became a friend at this time, perhaps recognising a fellow aristocrat.

The six-hour play was accepted by the director of Edinburgh Festival, Robert Ponsonby, and performed in the year he married his second wife: 1957 – in a cut version which did not do it justice and which was not well received. In his review Kenneth Tyman contrasted the play unfavourably with *Look Back in Anger*, which was first staged a year earlier. But the cast, including Robert Speaight, Michael MacLiammoir and Robert Eddison, believed strongly in the play which was directed by Christopher West and designed by Leslie Hurry, and said so at an unprecedented press conference. "You are the death and soul of the party" said MacLiammoir to a heckler. The cast also included Frank Thornton, Bernard Horsfall, Sebastian Shaw and Ronald Harwood (among contributors to this book), as well as Pauline Jameson and Derek Nimmo. *The Hidden King* may have been the final flowering of English Poetic Drama. Another admirer was a kilted bespectacled Edinburgh schoolboy who wrote to the author saying it was his favourite play since Shakespeare. This was Giles Gordon whose eponymous imprint was later to publish one of Griffin's books. A couple of years later another schoolboy, in London, was having difficulty with the Montherlant play he was studying for 'A' level and which he mentioned in section one of this introduction: the two schoolboys would enjoy swapping Griffin (and D.G. Bridson) anecdotes well into their middle age. Griffin and Bridson did not get on brilliantly well, but that's another story.

Writing *The Hidden King* opened the well-springs of Jonathan Griffin's poetic imagination. From the age of 50 his primary creativity went into writing poetry, as well as translating it – of which art and sullen craft he was an acknowledged master. As with Charles Reznikoff and other neglected older poets, several of his books came out at his own expense or from the small presses. Only very late in life was his work consecrated in a major list: that of the National Poetry Foundation in Maine who, at the recommendation of another old master, Carl Rakosi, brought out Griffin's *Collected Poems* in two volumes (amounting to 1000 pages) in 1989. America appreciated him more than England did. It was George Oppen, one of America's greatest poets, who wrote that "Griffin's syntax moves of its own force, moves in the force of the world, it restores light and space to poetry. It is what the poetry of England has lacked for – how long?"

11

Later the American poet and critic Eliot Weinberger wrote of Griffin, the hidden king: "He is something of a secret treasure; few of his stature are so little known .... The voice is unique .... rhythms like shattering glass; breath pauses presented through a system he has apparently invented. The music can be as dense as the later Bunting; the language as personal as that of David Jones .... It is a poetry of planetary consciousness .... the poet's response both ecstasy and rage. The intense lyrics in celebration of natural beauty – some of the loveliest in the language – are almost eclipsed by the bleak and apocalyptic meditations. Griffin is one of the few poets writing today who is confronting, *in the poem*, this earth of pesticides, deforestation, chemical waste".

Other admirers of Griffin's work include Ted Hughes and Jeff Nuttall. The latter wrote: "He is the only English poet I know who writes as frankly and eloquently about the suicide pact we call politics as, say, Ginsberg". Nuttall also wrote: "Light and air are not just subject to Griffin, they are materials as well. Thus his plea that imaginative play in the landscape might heal the landscape's poisoned state gains the credibility of any statement made by a man who's made a style out of the markings of his experience". A deeply religious agnostic, Griffin is an heir to the English spiritual tradition from Vaughan, Herbert and Traherne through to Hopkins – a major influence – and Edwin Muir. Of his own work, he has written: "Details of my own life are rather rare in my poems: I live it with zest but am short on the feeling that whatever has happened to me must interest other people .... Shame makes me write love poems to Earth and poems of solicitude for wronged posterity".

The green preoccupation and despair continued into his last – and still unpublished – book. It will be a while before this can be edited but parts of it should make their way into the eventual selected poems which he would have hated but which will secure his reputation in a way that a huge collected poems never can, desirable as it is to have this available.

Griffin was one of the masters in the renaissance of poetry translation over the last twenty years. He brought over work from many languages into English, finding his truest voice(s) in French and Portuguese: de Sena and Pessoa, Char and Mambrino. He particularly enjoyed collaborative work with his friend Susannah York on Claudel's play *Partage de Midi*. Two of his finest verse translations were Kleist's plays, *The Deep Man* and *The Prince of Homburg*, both starring Tom Courtenay. In 1986 Portugal invested him as a Knight of the Order of St. James of the Sword and in 1988 France followed suit with the Ordre des Arts et des Lettres. Among his papers are dozens of unpublished translations from several languages.

As he grew older and, unfortunately, deafer, his mien became ever more beatific, ever more angelic. He attended Kate's church, St. Mary's, Bourne Street, the house agnostic, much loved. He died on January 29, 1990. His funeral requiem mass was a musical and visual feast. If there is a heaven he will look the part, and will certainly be spending time listening to Schubert played by Schnabel, and discussing *The Hidden King* and *Mensagem* with Pessoa, whose English was excellent. But not at the same time. Music was *never* background for Jonathan Griffin. Nothing was. Because his time was spent in praise and because he lived a full and long life with "latefruit work" in abundance, his friends now celebrate rather than mourn. "The evening of life comes bearing its own lamp", wrote Joubert in a beautiful figure. For me, for all of us who loved him, Jonathan's sun stands always at noonday.

Editor's note
This text is based on a revised and uncut version of my obituary of Jonathan Griffin which appeared in *The Independent* on 30 January 1990 and on an obituary note which appeared in *Acumen* no. 11, 1990.

JONATHAN GRIFFIN

PARIS,
VE Day.

I have just been up the Champs Elysées to the Arc de
Triomphe and back. There could be no more right setting
for a popular festival on the grandest of scales. The crowd
is immense, yet there is still room to walk comfortably. It
is curiously quiet – very gay, a lot of shouting and
laughter and noise of aeroplanes and of hooters, but the
general impression is of hundreds of thousands of people
perfectly content just to stroll. There is not a wild and
single-minded search for alcohol; they are seeking something else, and it is exactly what they are finding, freedom
just to stroll in their streets and to rejoice in the thought of
the victory. London must have been just as wonderful, but
perhaps a bit differently; how was it? Did you go to Buck-
ingham Palace? I have stolen a little time to sit coolly in
the garden of the Maison des Alliés and begin this letter
to you before going out again to hear the Trocadero in
answer to one of the nicest invitations I have had – a
letter from Michèle Danjon which starts: "Papa et Mama
ne veulent pas que cette journée se passe sans vous avoir
vu ...." and goes on to ask me to join them at the Brissonnières' flat.

Last night, as the great story leaked out, rejoicings
began in the streets. Moyens took Bobbie, T.S. Elliot and
me for a drive around Paris, and already there was considerable gaiety on the Boulevards and in the Champs
Elysées, elsewhere being still quiet. Afterwards I visited
Lassaigne in his office, which looks right down the
Champs Elysées, and there we celebrated with champagne and cognac the fact that, having seen the start of
the war together, we were together for its close.

I have just seen a happy and rowdy band of gaily-
dressed young French people marching (more or less)
along the rue du Faubourg St. Honoré with a poster
saying "VIVE LE MARÉCHALE STALINE".

I will finish this letter tomorrow.

14

Last night was indeed gay. After leaving the Brissonnières' delightful party I went to the Etoile, where a wonderfully happy and yet gentle crowd was milling around the illuminated arch and shouting with pleasure at the fireworks. I ran into Desjardins, who took me off eventually on top of one of the radio cars to someone's flat, where Pierre Lefevre, Sturge Moore and others of RF's English team were gambolling drunkenly under the serene gaze of an enchanting water-colour of Marie's – Home on foot all down the Champs Elysées and through the Place de la Concorde, and to bed at 2 a.m.

Bobby is in good form. How nice it is to hear him say "splendid" again. He and I have been putting ourselves au courant with the theatre. The best thing we have seen is *Les Mal Aimés* of François Mauriac at the Comédie Française. As you know, I don't at all like Mauriac's view of life, because it is aimed at supporting an abdication of the individual's independence and because it degenerates into lachrymosity (as one sees all too clearly when he is writing political articles in the *Figaro*); but I am lost in admiration of the excellence, beauty even, of his sheer writing for the stage. The production was first-class. The other great pleasure was the film *Les Enfants du Paradis*. This is one of the great French films. It just goes on and on and on, there seems no reason why it should stop and one is content to go on sitting and watching it for hours. I won't describe it, for you will surely see it in London. Another marvel of defiance of the German occupation!

I must now leave this nice garden and collect Bobby. He and I are going to lunch with Guy Delapierre (who lives in the house where Racine died), and later we are going to visit Marie L.

Editor's note

It seemed appropriate to include something by Jonathan Griffin. So I sat myself down among the boxes of unpublished poems, translations, essays etc. etc. and enjoyed myself for a few hours. *Embarras de richesse*. I re-read some of his letters. The right one selected itself: the carbon copy of a letter written to someone from Paris on VE Day. Not all the names can be identified, at least not by me. But Moyens – it appears from another letter – was the young head of French Radio's foreign service music programmes. Bobby is Robert Speaight. T.S. Elliot is presumably T.S. Eliot. Marie in the first and last paragraph of the part of the letter written on May 9 is Marie Laurençin. Sturge Moore is Nicholas Moore's uncle. Other identifications on a postcard please.

RACHEL BLAU DUPLESSIS

from DRAFT 1: IT
in honor of Jonathan Griffin

No "books"   no ministers   no tow art
"no sandpoems"   build of it, not on it
it is sacred what you can do with it
the general aura of quest just as a baseline.
This silence awash with
bodies   flowered   aglow astripe to be
folded over signals.
Words' ribbon-wing hover, hovers, hovering.
Silence, silence, silence
was, this was, the implicit subject was
never foolhardy.

Silences are the reaches of discourse
(rich incipit's big initials)
                              walled
There is a yes and a no   up
                       welled
Sorrow? weeping yes and weeping no
it   is the definition of speaking;
gladness too is it, its weeping.
Silence is not the only subversion; it is.
The letters rise into a consuming which makes more
black fire flaming on white fire.
Fire fear (fears) fire. Scared is sacred.
Black arrow shot in blacker sleep
green word fold in greeny pock of folk
Speak, quiver, before your waves grow destitute
Dark feather dropped in foam of darker, antecedent sea.

KEITH BOSLEY

TELLING THE TRUTH
for Jonathan Griffin

When you arrived in heaven, I trust
that you were welcomed by the just
*   with a V sign:*
this was your gift to Europe when
we tried to hang our washing on
*   the Siegfried Line.*

Victory, yes, but Freedom too
in Dutch, you said, and this rings true
*   forty years later:*
Beethoven's Fifth – your Roman morse! –
on air declares it still in force
*   as* alma mater.

We took part in a conference
to build a bridge from here to France
*   between whose shores*
much lies: some truth was told at least.
You said my poem was a feast:
*   now it is yours.*

"What is truth?" Pilate asked, and hoped
the answer would be safely kept
        outside his province:
Messieurs, our question is germane
but we are not required to scan
        the silent heavens.

What kind of truth (so much we take
as read when culture is at stake)
        do poets tell?
Truth is not facts: our opposite
is lies, not fiction. Failing it
        we boil in hell.

18

For Baudelaire truth itself was hell
and Tasso languishing in jail
        was like those souls
whom waking nightmare kept from dream
because the Real stifled them
        within its walls.

But that reality of which
mankind cannot bear very much
        includes our own:
for us self-doubting Thomases
the film we see is not always
        the one being shown.

"Man is a poor conductor of
reality": Reverdy I love
        but wonder how
he left the world that was his oyster
and, godless, traded for the cloister
        the here and now.

Eluard could conduct the real
and earth it without burial:
        he even raised it
to where the sunlight overhead
was like a belly in a bed.
        When his friends praised it

he told them that his native land
was like a street without an end:
        when they protested
he saw that the Surrealist
joins worlds, but harder heads are just
        not interested.

"Truth is for systematic thinkers"
alas: we totter on the brink as
        we improvise
knowing "the newsboy and the number
seventy-three bus" with the lumber
        that waiting lies

to spring to life in poems, knowing
(a different verb for you) that flowing
          through us is time
moment to moment, hand to mouth
and we must plot the spirit's growth
          or turn to crime.

No wonder Existentialists
took overdoses, slashed their wrists:
          philosophers
faced with Racine's demand to make
something from nothing lie awake
          in the small hours.

We makers on the other hand
know daily what it is to stand
          before the abyss:
if we were systematic, we
would know too that philosophy
          was once like this.

"Too truthful. We poets must be
good liars", said Yeats, aware that he
          would upset Laura
Riding, who ditched the craft of verse
because truth goes from plain to worse
          with poetry's aura.

Rimbaud, she wrote, gave up because
his words were means: and yet in prose
          beyond romancing
he slung his ropes from tower to tower
flowers from a window, gold from a star
          and went on dancing.

That is our business, to connect
like Forster, even to transact
          from tongue to tongue
and then, like Mallarmé, to play
on lute or blue guitar and say
          what sense has sung.

But do we fiddle while Rome burns?
Not when a Finnish peasant turns
      to the same theme:
singing a boat built out of spells
"uncarved ... no shaving pared" he yells
      Come on, now dream!

Enter the poem: it will ask
participation in its task
      or else we lose.
All the best liturgies tell lies
to the outsider, so it is
      for us to choose.

The shaman mounts a stick of straw
calls it a horse: by the same law
      his lettered henchman
summons a sunset with a clause
or offers proof that Shakespeare was
      really a Frenchman.

Voilà le Rêve ... as Orpheus moved
trees and awoke the one he loved
      playing his crwth
till Homer, we are told, departed
from the official line and started
      telling the truth.

Messieurs and partners, once again
a tunnel is proposed between
      England and France:
we shall more easily enlighten
each other, which will doubtless heighten
      la différence.

We are all Alexandrians now:
Ecclesiastes shows you how
      irony rules
while we learn from Theocritus
to name the tame, maintaining thus
      old rituals.

                  April 1987

TOM COURTENAY

What a performance! So said Jonathan, standing wide-eyed and full of wonderment in the dressing-room doorway. You wondered how he had got there, all the way from Primrose Hill to Manchester, without Kathy to guide him. But get there he did, every performance but one (he missed a matinée one day) of Kleist's *The Prince of Homburg*, which he had translated from the German.

He was so very happy that his translation was being performed. After seeing it he almost invariably said 'What a performance'. Sometimes he paused a while before saying it, the finger-tips of each hand touching in contemplation, perhaps considering what else he might say. Sometimes after an especially lively evening he would give extra emphasis to the first word: 'WHAT a performance'. Occasionally, perhaps not wishing to repeat himself too often, he offered a slight variation: 'Now that was a performance'. But mostly it was 'What a performance'. And he meant it. His eyes twinkled and shone with excitement. He loved theatre and in particular the Royal Exchange Theatre of Manchester and it gave him great pleasure, through his activity as a translator, to be involved in the Exchange's work. 'One feels magic can happen in this building', he said.

I never met anyone who so struck me as being such a happy and unselfconscious intellectual. Who so loved what we are pleased to call The Arts.

He came to see me once in a thin farce I had foolishly got involved in. It was my unhappiest time in the theatre. There were other visitors in the dressing-room after the performance so Jonathan, who spoke quietly, did not manage to get a word in. I remember wondering what he had made of the evening, what he would say. Not being a quick mover, he was the last visitor to leave the dressing-room. Before departing he looked at me wide-eyed – with curiosity, if not with joy and wonderment: 'What a craftsman', he said, courteously. Thank you, Jonathan.

JONATHAN DELAMONT

For those of us still possessed of our quaint faith in the continuing value of the poetic vision, I think that Jonathan Griffin, one of the few post-war English poets who actually shows any sign of such faith or vision imbuing his poems, has to be regarded as an heoric figure. Mostly we seem to get this or that excuse for *not* having any faith in poetic vision, though written, paradoxically, in a semblance of poetry; or, conversely, a sort of shamanistic, crypto-pentecostal substitute for faith and vision, which can be possessed of considerable *frisson*, but which moves no mountains and proffers no sense of vision clearer than mud, even if it is Maenporth mud. Perhaps we would-be-poets, practitioners of 'Contemporary Verse', are not to be blamed: we have eschewed the complacent beliefs of our forebears, yet have nothing with which to replace them bar intellectual virtuosity and/or psychoshamanistic folderols; in which circumstances there is not much on which to base any sense of direction or of numinous supra-phenomenal reality. But this does not excuse us our duty to go on searching: and it was his impassioned heart-searching, though fortified with nothing more than an agnostic's faith-in-doubt, that allowed Jonathan Griffin to break through into something which looks suspiciously like great contemporary poetry, rather than contemporary verse: reading his poems is and should be a shaming experience if we are among those who have merely exchanged complacent belief for complacent unbelief. This latter syndrome is the one more than any other, on the intellectual plane, which subsequent generations will note when they weigh us in the balance and find us mostly wanting, however virtuosic or superficially inventive.

There are scores of points I would like to have raised with him: even if all is indeed always now, and in our mundane fragmentary scraps of space-time-bound consciousness we do in truth sit unsuspectingly in the midst of a thinly-veiled eternity, omnisciently and omnipresently stuck in the illusion of our egocentric transience, this does not help us if we are not attuned to the right waveband on the sub-ether radio which poets of all times and places use to contact their fellow-spirits in despite of only-apparent time and distance. If *I* am I am certainly not aware of it; but I'd venture to guess that if Jonathan Griffin were before us now, talking to poets and poetry enthusiasts about vital priorities, his testament would include the following points, more or less in this order:-

1)   You can be as atheistic as you like, but it gives you no right to complacency or cynicism: it needs no leap of faith to believe in the living earth, or to realise that at the very least devotion to, and care for, the endangered planet on which we live can and should fill any God-shaped gap inside us;

2)   You can unbelieve, and yet receive: there is no need to doubt the source of truly creative, poetic inner resource: it transcends the death of the Gods, or God, as eidola in which we might 'believe' or 'disbelieve'. There is therefore no call to conclude that 'poetry is no longer possible';

3)   If you cannot pull yourselves out of the vicious circle of complacency, cynicism and greed from which proceeds the steady self-destruction of Earth's ability to sustain life, you deserve and ought to become extinct, for the sake of all other species less devastating and more deserving of life;

4)   To verify the above, and perhaps other hidden truths as well, you need no extravagant degree of talent: about twenty-odd years of ruthless self-questioning and soul-search should suffice, coupled with enough determination in the following of your own star to be able to disregard all temptations sourced in literary fashion or conventional wisdom. Poetry is radical heartsearch, not avoidance of crux issues by means of irony or linguistic sorcery, however diverting these things may be.

The proof of the above assertions is there both explicitly and implicitly in Jonathan Griffin's poems, which therefore ought to be read and absorbed by anyone with any notion that he or she has the present and future of the poetry of poetry – as distinct from verse-linguistics – at heart. His own formidable intellect never seduced him away from urgent poetic necessity: this in itself is an object lesson to all other would-be-serious poets, in an epoch where education in intellectual facility has far outstripped common sense, let alone wisdom. I can think of no other contemporary poet who has so thoroughly and convincingly transcended the comfortable, complacent *ennui* of the cold-war period, seeking refuge neither in the distractions of the present, with all of its garish fairground-attractions, nor in imaginings, hankerings for a more poetically-conducive past, ancient or recent. He was a man of vast respect for European tradition; but he lived in the present and spoke up for the future. His poems will always be on my shelf, and his exemplary presence, I hope, somewhere close to my writing-arm.

CHRISTOPHER FRY

"Don't expect to find me in my poems" Jonathan wrote, as a first line to a poem in 1975, and it's true that they don't contain all of him. It would have been a great deal to contain in the spare strokes of his verse, but in the lean, gentle-voiced precision there is the recognizable man. The reticence and control of the poems are a part of him, the unspoken breadth of experience seems silently to inform them. In the thirty years during which from time to time I enjoyed his company it was only gradually, and in many ways very belatedly, that I could begin to measure the whole man. He never – I think *never* – spoke to me about what he had done. The military journalist was unheard of by me, the diplomat in the Paris embassy I scarcely heard-tell-of. What I knew was his pleasure and interest in every moment as it came, his warmth of heart, his quickly responsive sense of humour – the laughter we had, Jonathan, Kate, my wife and I, along the sea-front at Aldeburgh between bouts of music. It seemed to me that in his thin, strong-shouldered height and his visionary face, there was something legendary, a thoroughly rational Quixote, so it was only fitting that, as reward for his translations of Pessoa and Camoens, he should receive the Order of St. James of the Sword and for his French translations become a Chevalier de l'Ordre des Arts et des Lettres.

FR. JOHN GILLING

In one of his poems Jonathan wrote 'Religion will not go away.' This was certainly true for him, as for many who would call themselves agnostics. The people of this church would see him at Mass on Sunday and on the great holy days of the year: he would talk to them with affection and courtesy – especially to strangers and young people who might feel shy or unwanted: Kate and Jonathan would welcome us to their home to meet their other friends, and would come and help support every kind of parish activity from Bible studies to opera productions. Noone could be more appreciative than Jonathan was of good church music well-sung and well-played, or of a decent sermon. So he made us all feel better and be better. You could say of him, as Auden said on meeting Charles Williams, 'He made you feel twice as tall, twice as intelligent and twice as good-looking.' And I remember Auden going on to say 'I think he was the only saint I have known.'

I have no authority to claim sanctity for Jonathan nor really to talk of his beliefs. But there can be no doubt, however far he may have been from Christian orthodoxy, that he had a great sense of the holy, especially of the holiness of creation, a doctrine too often neglected in the orthodox Christianity of the churches. Jonathan's sense of the holiness of things and of people informed his writing and gave grace to his life among us: to him the world has always been sacred and of absolute value. This was the fount and origin of his courtesy.

It was also this awareness which made him acutely sensible to evil, to the exploitation and manipulation of things and people in greed and pride. He was no Christian Scientist: he saw the reality of evil and the vulnerability of the good.

I would guess that it was this which made him so faithful in his attendance at Mass. For in the Mass we recall and represent the sacrifice in love and in courtesy for the world of one human being whom we believe is also the beginning and the end of all creation. In the Mass we see the costly triumph of good over evil, of life against death and by the Mass we enter into the same sacrifice with awe and with joy, with fear and with hope, above all with thanksgiving. By holy communion we are united with Christ and through Him with all our brothers and sisters living and departed this life.

Jonathan was thus in the great English spiritual tradition of the affirmative way – Julian of Norwich, Thomas Traherne, William Blake, Wordsworth, Hopkins, Muir – that way which knows God through his creation. As we pray at this Mass for those who will feel his loss most deeply we pray for him that he may this day find what he sought: 'The love that moves the sun and all the stars.'

Spoken at Jonathan Griffin's requiem mass
St Mary the Virgin
Bourne Street
7th February, 1990

GILES GORDON

Jonathan Griffin – how exotic the name seemed to a 17-year-old Scot; how heraldic; so romantic that it might be pseudonymous – was the first author I met. He was also the first author to inscribe a book to me. The flyleaf of my copy of *The Hidden King*, somewhat battered now and much reread, is embellished in Jonathan's spidery scrawl in his inevitable mundane blue biro:

> For Giles Gordon
> whose fresh approach and
> warm response encouraged
> not only me but the whole
> cast at Edinburgh in 1957;
> gratefully.
> > Jonathan Griffin.

Born and bred in Edinburgh, I was theatre-struck. The International Festival each August was the three weeks to wait for, and nothing ruined my summer more than when my parents booked a family holiday which meant, as in some years it did, that I'd miss a week or even two of nirvana.

I had a particular addiction to the Church of Scotland's Assembly Hall at the top of the Mound which, each Festival for three carnival weeks, was transmogrified into a playhouse, with thrust apron stage devised years before by Tyrone Guthrie. The intimacy this theatre afforded between actors and audience was thrilling, pulsating. I had, prior to 1957, seen a number of productions there, usually try-outs by the Old Vic on the way to Waterloo Road. I remember a springy *Twelfth Night*, with John Neville as a palsied Aguecheek. I especially remember sitting in a front row pew, a fleshy male bottom clad in stretched black tights pronouncing a soliloquy in a dreamy nasal Welsh voice above me, and I was not impressed as the proximity of the buttocks to my face distracted from the poetry. This was Richard Burton essaying Hamlet. I also remember, with considerably more enthusiasm, Tyrone Guthrie's gloriously rich and inventive production of Sir

David Lyndsay's *The Thrie Estaites*, a kaleidoscope of medieval Scotland come to life featuring most of the
country's best actors including Duncan Macrae, Tom
Fleming and John Cairney. The whole thing was a political orgy, Hieronymous Bosch translated.

Thus it was disappointing to learn early in 1957 that
there would only be one production at the Assembly Hall
that Festival (in previous years there had been two or
more) and that it would not be a Shakespeare, it wouldn't
even be a classic. Aged 17, I only really approved of the
"classics", for they had stood the test of time. Anyone, in
a sense, could write a new play, and I wanted something
special. The new play, by a hitherto unknown dramatist
and poet (at least in Scotland) was being mounted for
three weeks because it was so expensive to put on, and
was the first major dramatic production at the Festival to
be presented by the Festival Society itself (albeit in association with the impresario Stephen Mitchell).

The Hidden King opened to what I hope are as bad
reviews as any play can have received – that is, I hope no
playwright ever received a more severe verbal beating
than poor Jonathan did. Kenneth Tynan particularly dis-
dained it. On the other hand, J C Trewin, that sound ap-
praiser of literary excellence, albeit in largely unread
publications, much admired it. Having read some of the
appalling notices, I went expecting the worst, and had
what is probably the most utterly engrossing and enrich-
ing evening I've spent in a theatre, and many of my most
memorable evenings have been spent there (though not
in recent years).

I shall assume that anyone reading these words is
probably familiar with Jonathan's masterpiece, and suffice
to remind that the "poem for the stage in the form of a
trilogy" opens with a prologue set in Portugal in 1578,
then moves to Spain. Act One is set in Venice and Padua
in the summer of 1598 (and how the light dazzled in
Christopher West's glorious production against Leslie
Hurry's sumptuous yet unfustian sets and costumes). Act
Two, during 1599 and 1600, roams around Venice and
Florence. Act Three mostly takes place three years later at
a Spanish port near Portugal. The settings, the time span,
the dramatist's vision and historical imagination, were in-

deed Shakespearian, as was the text which, mainly in verse but with shots of prose, was a sinuous, flexible instrument, stimulating lives to flower and fade, hopes to be raised and lowered, individuals to love and despair. It was a cornucopia of all life.

They do not, certainly not at the RSC or the RNT (neither of which had its being in 1957), make casts like this any more but the actors included Iain Cuthbertson, Frank Thornton, Derek Nimmo, John Bennett, Michael MacLiammoir (sulphurously sinister), Ronald Harwood, Hugh Cross, Bernard Horsfall, Clare Austin, Rosalind Atkinson, Sebastian Shaw (a lecherous villain), Beth Boyd, Richard Dare, Ernest Thesiger (the most emaciated, glittering, corrupt Cardinal imaginable), Pauline Jameson (radiance itself). In the leads were Robert Speaight, who gave the play rather a good write up in *The Tablet*, and the ethereal, Christ-like Robert Eddison as Dom Sebastian, claiming to be the King of Portugal, generally assumed to have been killed at the battle of Alcazar, twenty years earlier.

I cannot, at this distance in time, recall whether "Bobby" Speaight, as I wouldn't have dreamed of calling him, was theatre critic of *The Tablet* (I think he was but how did he cope with reviewing the plays in which he appeared, and when he wasn't "resting" how did he manage to see other plays?) or simply a regular columnist but I do remember that, in his article about the excitement which the production of *The Hidden King* generated, he remarked that *some* people were enthusiastic about it, including the saintly John Trewin and someone described as "a straightforward ordinary schoolboy," and a remark years later in Speaight's autobiography perpetuates the appelation. The description smarted at the time and smarts even more now. Maybe had I not, of course, been wearing my kilt when I attended the performance with the Griffins I mightn't have been solemnised so dully. On the other hand, Speaight was a Roman Catholic and perhaps any descendant of John Knox might have been regarded as "straightforward" and "ordinary", and there was no denying I was a schoolboy.

Who cares about the critics? (Certainly I never did when I became one, at *The Spectator*, a quarter of a

31

century later.) I'd read in an Edinburgh newspaper that Jonathan Griffin was in Edinburgh for the premiere of his play. I wrote him a letter, telling him how good his play was, and that he really wasn't to worry about the critics who were clearly morons. Unable to find a door that opened at the Assembly Hall during the day, I pinned my note – not thinking of Luther and the church door at Wittenberg – to a barred entrance of the Assembly Hall, watched by the statue of dour bedraggled old John Knox as I did so, and hoped that my envelope would reach Mr Griffin.

I can't remember, 35 years later, whether I received Jonathan's letter the next day or the day after. It was written in the hand, the blue biro, on the unheaded, slightly shiny ivory small paper I was to know so well in the years that followed. "Dear Mr Gordon", it began, and went on to express its gratitude for my response to the play, without – typical Jonathan – a word in response to my indignation about the critics. I remember feeling dizzy, nearly fainting (I can recall the thrill of reading the letter now) at Jonathan's suggestion – nay, assumption – that I accompany him and his wife to a matinée of the play within the next few days.

The day came, but I cannot, to my shame, remember anything about that second performance, so in awe was I of sitting next to playwright and wife (yet whether I sat between Jonathan or Kathleen or next to one of them I cannot recall). Jonathan was 51 during the year of *The Hidden King* (his friend Roger Senhouse, Lytton Strachey's last great love, had published the text at Secker & Warburg in 1955) and, I learned from the obituaries in 1990, only married Kathy that year. (I admit to having contributed heavily to the one in the *Daily Telegraph*).

To me at 17, Jonathan at 51 was as old (or as young) as he was when I was 49 and he in his 83rd and last year. Presumably he had fewer wrinkles, and certainly he was less stooped than he became, but he was, physically, essentially the same. Dressed in a light-coloured summer suit, thin, tall and ascetic-looking, with sandy hair disappeared from the centre of his head and improbably presenting a witty bald pate, his National Health-style spectacles made him seem at first look like a cultivated schoolboy. You had to listen hard to hear Jonathan's pearls of wisdom. He made no effort to raise his voice, to be heard above the clamour, either of the crowd or of the dinner table. Yet when he spoke, such was his natural authority and conviction, that everyone around went silent. In his later years I found his inability to countenance any view other than his own somewhat ennervating but when I first knew him, with his eyes so frequently a-sparkle, being with him was like quaffing the finest champagne.

After the performance, he and Kathy took me back stage to meet the actors. They weren't, of course, interested (except, I remember, Michael MacLiammoir, who, with mascara sweating all over his pocked unwholesome visage, was too interested) as they wanted, merely, to steal a few minutes' relaxation between matinée and evening performances: the production, when it opened, ran for nearly four hours. By the second time I saw it it had been shorn of, I think, nearly an hour and was artistically diminished.

A few days later Jonathan and Kathy came and had lunch at my parents' home, an event which I think went off painlessly. Everyone was terribly polite to everyone else.

Then began a correspondence between Jonathan and me – "Dear Mr Griffin"; "Dear Mr Gordon" – which lasted for five years until I came to live and work in London. Ten or twelve letters must have been exchanged before Jonathan dared "Dear Giles (if I may)" and a few letters more from me before I was invited to call him Jonathan. I still have, somewhere, all or most of his letters. They were an illuminating crash course in drama, with particular reference to the minor (and major, but Jonathan had a relish for – not the second rate but the less fashionable, the less well-known) Elizabethan and Jacobean playwrights. I dread to think what I wrote to him but, irrespective, the sweet, selfless man continued to undertake my theatrical education. "You really should read *The Dutch Courtesan*", I remember him instructing. The trouble was, and is, that I have always preferred plays in the playhouse to the naked texts in the study, which no doubt says all too much about my frivolity.

Jonathan tried to persuade me of the riches of opera but I was unconvinced: a mélange of art forms by those who can't achieve complete success with any one of them, I sullenly wrote back. Quietly he admonished in his next letter: you will come to appreciate opera when you are older. This, of course, irritated me but, as usual (though not always), he was right.

When I came to live and work in London in 1962, for his own publishers (Secker & Warburg) he and Kathy invited me and my (then) wife to dinner at their jewel-box of a house in Markham Street, Chelsea, before King's Road had become something approximating a seaside pier. The white terraced house was a feast of theatrical, operatic, poetic and literary *objets*, a sort of miniature, personalised Garrick Club. Did Kathy, with cats in tow, always serve fish? So I remember it. My memory of Jonathan, no doubt unfair, is of his talking and talking, blinking and smiling like a vole presiding over the meal of a lifetime, brooking comment from his guests without much enthusiasm. Not that he was rude – on the contrary – but that any guest who made a pitch for a paragraph or two would not always be encouraged. You could ask Jonathan what he thought of, say, *Love's Labour's Lost* at Stratford that season but you might find it difficult to make your point if you ventured to disagree with him and tried to express a contrary view to his.

As the years went by, I saw less of Jonathan and Kathy, especially – rather surprisingly – when they came to live near us, in Sharpleshall Street. When exercising a child or two on Primrose Hill, I would often see Jonathan striding across the public park in a world of his own. He maintained a cracking pace until a few years before he died. Sometimes I would accost him on Primrose Hill, much to my children's annoyance, and Jonathan would conduct a highflown conversation or virtual monologue, about the latest production at Stratford or Covent Garden, completely – but completely – ignoring the children. He came to exclude from his life what he wanted to exclude, and that was all but art and his friends.

In the last few years, we only exchanged Christmas cards. "We *must* get together next year. Love Jonathan and Kathy." But most years we didn't.

I have two small mementoes of him. First, at an auction at the National Theatre a decade or more ago I bought a watercolour costume design by Leslie Hurry of the Venetian Ambassador to Portugal in *The Hidden King*. The character does not appear to be listed among the dramatis personae; but no matter. Second, in 1963, after Fred Warburg had, more or less, ordered his partner Roger Senhouse to exile himself from Secker & Warburg (Roger had published a collection of Jonathan's poems, *The Rebirth of Pride*, in 1957), I had the privilege of publishing, in 1963, from my bedsitter in Ridgmount Gardens, a pamphlet of elegant poems by Jonathan, *The Oath and other poems*. It was the smallest repayment of an impossible debt.

JOHN GREENHALGH

I did not meet Jonathan until what was to become the final decade of his life. It was my loss that the acquaintance was made so late in the day. My memory must be that of many of his friends: apart from poetry, the seemingly endless talks about music and musicians. Jonathan's taste in music was catholic, his appreciation of artists discriminating. We shared an unswerving devotion to Schnabel with whom he had studied before the Second World War.

Music permeated his life. "Is poetry but an aspect of music?" I teased him. He was too modest to believe his creative facility as a poet could exceed the interpretative facility of the performer. It was Jonathan who, during the War, spotted the rhythmic connection between the opening bars of Beethoven's Fifth Symphony and the morse code for the letter 'V' – for Victory – which, subliminally, over many radio waves, attacked fascism as effectively as any cipher.

His unfailing courtesy could be seen on every level of communication. He borrowed a recording of some Webern and Boulez piano music from me. "I'll need to keep it a little longer than usual," he said. "It's simply not fair to inflict *this* music on Kate!" What of us? What did we inflict on *him*? Impossible to say, of course, so exceptional were his fine manners.

That Jonathan was a gentleman was axiomatic; he was also an intellectual in the true, humanist sense: *homo qui non facile definit.* The absence of any kind of judgmentalism in his nature was striking. Through this shone out the *anima naturaliter Christiana.* When challenged, more perhaps in terms of religious philosophy than theology, he would toy with those Greek negations, atheism and agnosticism, but essentially, as he refused to categorise others, so he accepted no categories for himself.

The Christian Church failed to hold him to a pattern of worship until his 75th year when he started to attend Sunday Mass in the Church of St Mary, Bourne Street and to join in its life. It was not fitting that this Griffin should die separated from his ancestral faith, and our *Vale* to him took place in the liturgical context of a Requiem Mass. How appropriate, too, that he should leave the church and people whom he had come to love and with whom he had chosen to identify himself to the strains of the *Pie Jesu* of Gabriel Fauré – a francophile to the end, indeed!

Tall; stooping; gold-rimmed spectacles; a voice so quiet you had to lean close to catch the precision of his Edwardian diction. When he laughed he giggled. A poet, an English poet; an enthusiast, an English enthusiast.

1956. Edinburgh Festival. *The Hidden King.* A long verse drama, in keeping with Fry and Eliot, about a lost King of Portugal. Starry cast: Robert Eddison, Sebastian Shaw, Micheál MacLiammoir, Robert Speaight, Ernest Thesiger, Pauline Jameson and then among the rest of us Derek Nimmo, Frank Thornton, John Bennett, me. Designed by Leslie Hurry. Presented by the wittiest, sweetest, gentlest of impresarios, Stephen Mitchell. The director was Christopher West from Covent Garden which tells all. Very grand. Very pre-Osborne.

Early rehearsals. MacLiammoir approaches a group of the rest of us. 'Now,' he says, 'you're a bunch of clever fellows. What the hell does this mean?' He points to a line in the text, something like: "And with arms outstretched the Pope laminates the epithalamium". We share MacLiammoir's bewilderment.

Someone says, 'The author's sitting over there, why not ask him?'

'Good idea,' says MacLiammoir and glides across to Jonathan, perched on a bentwood chair, legs curled one round the other, deeply engrossed as only he could be. MacLiammoir leans close to catch the precise Edwardian diction. They talk for ten minutes. MacLiammoir nods, retreats, glides back towards us and, in passing, murmurs, 'He doesn't know either.' It became the catchphrase of the production. 'Do stop laminating your epithalamium, you'll go blind.' Jonathan giggles rather than laughs.

Yes, an enthusiast; no, more than that, a devotee, a disciple. Going but once to a theatre or a concert hall or an art gallery was never enough. He'd see a play four, five times, perhaps more, delight in the subtlest variation of performance. Even a Japanese *No* play during a World Theatre Season in London. Had he really sat through it so many times? He'd imitate the different lengths of sound he'd detected in an unintelligible, gutteral howl from one of the actors. We laughed rather than giggled.

He and Kathy, his wife, like naughty adolescents caught holding hands, sharing pleasure, enthusiasms, gossip, insights. Wonderful hosts, good wine, good food, good chat.

Above all genuine modesty anchored to the highest standards both for himself and others. He'd studied the Beethoven piano sonatas with Artur Schnabel but afterwards played no more, aware of his relative shortcomings.

When he gave praise you felt it was worth something. When he received praise, he flushed, his eyes twinkled. He'd murmur 'I say!', astonished and grateful.

An impression that he'd been born out of his time. Hear him talk of his childhood in Berkshire, canoeing on a summer day, senses acute, awareness of a hushed and tranquil world before the war to end wars.

An amateur in the true meaning. A lover of art, a lover of beauty. Cultured in a way that probably no longer exists and even when it did was rare. An English poet, an English gent. A friend.

PETER HILEY

To be invited to write about Jonathan is a two-edged compliment – a great honour to be asked, but a quandary, how does one condense one's feelings about someone as multi-faceted as he was?

Poet, playwright, translator, wordsmith, sage, patron, critic, connoisseur of every form of art, wit, friend – a man of infinite gifts, who would have been as much at home in the 18th century, as the 20th.

For me the dominant memories are of humour, humanity and all-embracing friendship. As a friend, he had the wonderful ability, when occasion demanded, not just to suffer fools gladly, but to transform them into believing themselves sparkling companions – and thereby giving them a great uplift of spirit.

Jonathan was epitomised for me by the typical experience of meeting him in the interval of an opera or play, to be greeted with "What about THAT?" The only answer could be "WELL!", passing the ball back to him, to find out whether the 'that' was inspired by ecstasy from the music, or impish glee at the grotesquery of the costumes or a slipped wig. Either way his delight was infectious.

His knowledge and judgement on every aspect of art and literature were awe-inspiring. However obscure an opera, he would have seen it in some remote opera house in the only production this century, and he was able to recall every detail.

But even more importantly than his being a walking encyclopaedia of the arts was his immense capacity for friendship, and his enquiring and attentive interest in whomever he met, swans or geese, (and making swans of us all).

Although unfettered by any need to understand too much about the detailed mechanics or complexities of modern life, the motor-car for example or kitchen gadgetry, he was deeply aware of and bothered by man's ruination of his environment, and he was 'green' long before the arrival of today's meaning.

Despite his being shocked by ugliness and pollution and any form of inhumanity, I felt him to be a man of happiness, able to devote his life to his 'own thing' – his own many things – which he did with such compelling and infectious enthusiasm, as to carry his friends with him, and we will always remember him with love and respect and a great big smile.

ROLAND HILL

Jonathan Griffin always seemed to me to embody Cardinal Newman's definition of a gentleman: someone who never inflicts pain. But there was nothing Victorian or saintly about his kind of *gentillesse*. It combined courtesy and elegance, a Chaucerian and Shakespearian love of this world and awareness of its bewitching power. Knowing Jonathan was to know what Tertullian meant by "anima naturaliter Christiana", the Stoic's idea that knowledge of God is implanted in man's soul from the outset and can be diminished but never eradicated: it is man's natural *ambiente* – part of his being. Jonathan eventually, and undoubtedly through Kate, who was so much the "driver" in their wonderful union, found a spiritual home in the Anglo-Catholic world of St. Mary the Virgin, Bourne Street, SW1. Surely, the clouds of incense that enveloped all at his Requiem Mass carried his soul to its eternal rest.

He was a modern poet, down to earth politically, aware of the corrupting effect of absolute power. This may have induced an unconscious affinity with the German dramatist and essayist Heinrich von Kleist whose *Prince of Homburg* he translated so well and was fortunate to have performed in 1980 in a fine production at the Manchester Royal Exchange Theatre. The Prussian Prince values the claims of the heart more than the claims of reason and military duty. The author's vision, however, also anticipates some of a later age's psychological insights into the confusions to which the heart is prone.

Jonathan Griffin's own *The Hidden King* is a drama for our time. Unfortunately, whether because of its poetic form or the profundity of its message, its excellent staging at the 1957 Edinburgh Festival failed to find the acclaim it deserved. The English theatre was tired of its T.S. Eliots and Christopher Frys and seemed to want nothing so much as to escape to the angry realism and the insular domestic comforts of the kitchen sink. "If he is not the King, is he a King?" Jonathan Griffin asks, "and if the King, has he become a King? There is a hidden king in each of us and we are all impostors." The mystery of the stranger who surfaced in Venice in the late sixteenth century is left open. Is he the missing King Sebastian of Portugal, believed to have died twenty years earlier at the battle of Alcazar? Or is he vicariously embracing the martyr's crown for the sake of his country suffering under Spanish rule? The theme is the strength that comes from weakness.

In one of his poems Jonathan speaks of his life and work as the "nearest thing to an agnostic's prayer". His pride, he emphasised, was in the contrast between his art and his life. And he warned: "Don't expect to find me in my poems." But we are entitled to remember him as he was, the lovable man who had no enemies, who contentedly sat in his chair stroking a no less contented cat on his lap. He liked the good things in life – wine, food, conversation, friendship and music, which perhaps answered most closely to his idea of God. He was enthusiastic for anything he was doing, whether producing a play, writing, talking, and he had a genuine interest in others. His dear Kate, so busy and full of life and thoughts could not have been more different yet they were that rarest of couples, truly "one in heart and soul".

BRIAN HORNE

The first book Jonathan Griffin gave me was one of his own: the collection of poems published in 1981 by The Menard Press called *The Fact of Music*. In his delicate, spidery handwriting he inscribed it

> To
> Dr. Brian Horne
> with
> eagerness and diffidence
> mixed
> > Jonathan
> > 12. vii. 81

The words were placed, in relation to one another, and in relation to the title around which they were arranged, as carefully and precisely as in any of the poems that followed. He intended them to be read in a particular way and he made sure that they were. The gift itself and the style of the giving were characteristic of the man who gave it. In his life, as in his art, manner and matter were fused. There was also, in this instance, a combination of playfulness and honesty that I came to recognize as part of the essence of his personality. 'Eagerness and diffidence – mixed.' Far from flattering me, and increasing the sense of my own importance, the words startled me into humility. I soon realised that this was the effect he had on many people. The eagerness was not an outward expression of an inward desire for acceptance or praise; nor was the diffidence rooted in an uncertainty about the quality of his work. He did not flatter, but simply and unaffectedly, valued and respected others and anticipated in them – without arousing guilt or resentment – standards of intelligence, generosity and honesty that were his own. It came as a surprise to many, accustomed to a world of casual acquaintances and trivial exchanges in which words are often substitutes for feelings and verbal forms hide more than they reveal, to encounter such translucency and be taken so seriously.

In that astonishing work of the fifth century, *The City of*

God, St Augustine imagines two cities: *civitas dei* and *civitas terrena*, and describes the laws governing these two societies. The law of the one is generosity (in its deepest sense), the law of its opposite is envy. Jonathan was a citizen of that city which lived by the law of generosity, the city of God. This generosity was not naive, nor even innocent; accompanying it was an anger directed at all who lived by the law of envy. To those who had met only the eager and diffident Jonathan Griffin, the man who seemed to find delight in the smallest particulars of life, the ferocity of the anger in the poetry came as a shock. But it was a vital part of him: poems like *Full Fresh* and *Suspension* are to be read in the context of others like *You who Avoid the Issue* and *The Makers of the Amazon Desert*. What is remarkable is that the rage is controlled, not by will, but by artistry. The style of the verse, the very arrangement of the words on the page, is both the channel of the anger and the instrument by which it is contained. He denounced greed, cruelty, wilful stupidity and lies almost as fiercely as the great Augustine himself; but his vision of the future, our future and that of the planet, was more ambiguous – even though the manner of his life, paradoxically, could be read as a concrete manifestation of the virtue of hope. I once had the temerity to write to him: "I dare to suggest, Jonathan, that we may be seen as mirror-images: I, a believer, live on the edge of doubt; you, a sceptic, are in love with belief". He acknowledged and enjoyed the irony.

BERNARD AND JANE HORSFALL

Jonathan was a gentle giant. The sheer mass of his life experience is awe inspiring. For a pianist turned journalist turned military adviser turned Director of BBC European Intelligence turned diplomat he didn't do badly to have been made a Portuguese Knight for his translations of Pessoa, to have so many major works of translation published and performed, to have his first major verse play *The Hidden King* put on at the Edinburgh Festival with a brilliant cast, and finally to have the massive rich harvest of his verse published in two thick volumes.

He was a heroic explorer and an agent for life's growth, blessed with his supportive, provocative, cajoling, life-enhancing wife Kathy. We fortunately knew them together over many years. What dinners. What friends. What talk. What jokes. What wine. Jonathan never closed himself off. He always listened, always paid the closest attention to whatever was in the air. Patient, compassionate, an understander of darkness and a knower of turmoil, he would, to quote loosely from his Foreword to the first volume of his poems, bring discipline, clarity and resonance to whatever he said, as much as to whatever he wrote. For us he could radiate a light of understanding. In private and in public he took such care because he cared so much. He chose and rehearsed his own public readings assiduously. "I don't want people to be bored!" And he'd launch himself, sometimes a little nervously to begin with, into his work, and gather confidence, and soon hook us all into the closest attention to his deepest concerns. That dear lanky fellow with those small gold specs. How we love him.

He seemed a fearful man who was unafraid, a gentle man who was angry, a deeply serious man who laughed a lot, a humble man who was a hero, a quiet man who raged, a very knowledgeable man who was so human, concerned and caring as much for individuals as for the human race, imbued with History yet with a young and forward-looking mind. His lyrical poetry dances but his warnings thunder. A great story teller, full of surprises and a wicked sense of fun and a great relish for life. An agnostic who was surely touched with the Grace of God. And how he loved his cats.

PETER HOY / RENÉ CHAR

BLUE BEACON

Not near that blue light that comes
from your dress may my flesh
like a duped sail revile a false wind!

Maris Stella, I kiss
the warmth that hides in your face,
star which like Sirius flushes,

which mans me, – whom with a cry
I take, with such love as has always
defied the very constellations.

Translated by Peter Hoy

LES TROIS SŒURS

Mon amour à la robe de phare bleu,
je baise la fièvre de ton visage
où couche la lumière qui jouit en secret.

J'aime et je sanglote. Je suis vivant
et c'est ton cœur cette Étoile du Matin
à la durée victorieuse qui rougit avant
de rompre le combat des Constellations.

Hors de toi, que ma chair devienne la voile
qui répugne au vent.

René Char s'est voué continûment à la célébration ardente et violente de la Beauté. Dans sa langue, *amour* veut dire *poésie*, celle qui déstabilise le soleil et la terre, exige lucidité et rigueur, force les limites de la terre.

Jonathan n'a jamais cessé de regarder fixement cette poésie faite d'éclairs et d'offenses, de résistance et d'effraction.

Et cette poésie-là n'a jamais été aussi bien *lue* : aucune alluvion, aucune parure, aucun souffle importé, rien que cette voix de silex, de ronces.

Même souffle, même amour.

FR. FREDERICK JACKSON SSC

*'Hence it is that it is almost a definition of a gentle-
man to say that he is one who never inflicts
pain....He has his eyes on all his company; he is ten-
der towards the bashful, gentle toward the distant,
merciful towards the absurd; he can recollect to
whom he is speaking; he guards against unseasonable allusions to topics which may irritate; he is seldom prominent in conversation, and never
wearisome. He makes light of favours while he does
them, and seems to be receiving when he is confer-
ring. He never speaks of himself except when com-
pelled, never defends himself by mere retort, he has
no ears for slander or gossip, is scrupulous in imput-
ing motives to those who interfere with him, and in-
terprets everything for the best.'*

J H Newman

Newman's definition of a gentleman might have been
written for Jonathan Griffin.

I first met Jonathan at S. Mary's church, Bourne St.
SW1, some fourteen years or so ago now at one of those
exotic liturgical feasts which S. Mary's, with just a hint of
'folie de grandeur', does so well. He had accompanied
Kate to the Mass as he often did and we met briefly at the
drinks party afterwards. I remember a pair of very old-
fashioned sandals, two bright and gently understanding
eyes, and on leaving him feeling twice as big as I was. It
is in the nature of true greatness not to leave the impression that one is oneself great but rather that the other person is, and this Jonathan always did. Such was his
humility and integrity and understanding that one always
came from him feeling enriched and twice as big as before.

Our second meeting was by chance at a bus-stop outside Foyles Bookshop in the Charing Cross Road. Less
than a minute after meeting we were totally absorbed in
discussing T. S. Eliot's use of objective correlatives –
buses, tourists, shoppers, traffic and noise all quite

49

forgotten. Jonathan had this capacity to draw one into his own enthusiasm and excitement. When with him it was as natural to talk about Eliot's use of language at a busy bus-stop in the Charing Cross Road as it would have been the weather in the Crush Bar at Covent Garden.

Thus began a friendship that will always be a very special part of my own private 'Sursum Corda'.

A poet is essentially a contemplative and sifts beneath the surface of things to listen to the inexpressible and echo it in language. When all we who have known Jonathan are dead too those in the future will know him still through his poetry and the echoing there of those values which lie beneath the surface of things and to which he listened and echoed with such gentleness and courtesy and integrity. But to their loss they will never be able to hold the treasure of his friendship in their hearts as we do.

St. Paul ended his letter to the Church at Philippi by writing:

> *Finally, brethren, whatever is true, whatever is honourable, whatever is just, whatever is pure, whatever is lovely, whatever is gracious, if there is any excellence, if there is anything worthy of praise, think upon these things. What you have learned and received and heard and seen in me, do; and the God of peace will be with you.*

And I am convinced that the God of peace, whom Jonathan knew under other forms and different names, is with him now and has him safely enfolded in His arms.

And they're very probably talking about objective correlatives.

IVAN JELINEK

With Jonathan's demise, I have lost a dear and trusted friend. But first of all, how, where and under what circumstances did we meet?

Prague, 1939, Munich crisis, general mobilisation.

At that time I worked at the Prague Short Wave Station. I was responsible for programmes in Czech, English, French and Spanish. Immediately after President Beneš had offered our despairing country its last hope by proclaiming general mobilisation, the foreign press arrived in our offices.

Five individuals were waiting for me in the entrance hall, two of them women. One of the men explained that they were in Prague to report on local events for their newspapers, that they would like to arrange a regular time for their daily reports, and would the Short Wave Station oblige by connecting them with New York, London.

"..and Paris," said a man in Czech who was standing somewhat apart from the two couples. "I'm Beuve-Méry,[1]" he went on, "a French journalist. I have a Moravian wife and so I speak Czech."

He turned to the two English-speaking couples, "Would you allow me to settle our business with this gentleman? It'll be quicker."

"You see, Dr. Safránek of your Ministry of Foreign Affairs sent us to you....they just shrugged their shoulders....so if you would help us....we've arranged for our despatches to be received in our respective countries at whatever time you would be kind enough to allow us..a quarter of an hour daily, while the crisis lasts..and I can assure you that our reports are bound to help your cause in our countries....in France, England and America...", he continued in English. "This is Jonathan Griffin and his wife Joan from London....and this is Vincent Sheean[2] and his wife from New York."

I explained that I had to tell the Chairman, Dr. Šourek, about their request, which I personally would be happy to grant; and if Dr. Šourek were agreeable, I would then have to consult the Chief Engineer about the technicalities, and then alert the boss of the Short Wave Station.

Within seconds I was knocking on the door of the Chairman's office and dashed in without waiting to be asked.

"I'm in luck, sir," I said, "you told me once not to hesitate to come to you so long as it was a serious matter."

I explained, the Chairman listened carefully, obviously nervous. "Do as you see fit..you can tell everyone that I've given you the green light."

I went to the Chief Engineer. No trouble at all, he said at once. I walked upstairs to warn the boss. He turned pale and said he hoped I knew what I was doing...still, he would not interfere.... I ran downstairs to my guests. Sheean wanted his slot late at night, while both Griffin and Beuve-Méry asked for their fifteen minutes early in the evening, if possible.

When times had been agreed, I confirmed the arrangements with the Chief Engineer. This part of the operation took just a few minutes. Then they all rushed away saying that they would be back in good time for their transmissions the same night.

Some time after seven Jonathan Griffin, holding the door open for his wife, stepped inaudibly on his yellow rubber soles into the reception hall, where I had been waiting for him.

"Yes," said Jonathan Griffin, "I have my first report ready..and it won't be a plea for appeasement...."

He stood there for a moment, making his characteristic head movements as if pecking at some invisible grain that hovered in front of his nose, his eyes hidden by small, steel-rimmed glasses. He stood there, thin, nervous, gentle and direct, looking much the same as in later years, in a position at last to express his contempt of the British Government's policy and give his impressions of what was happening. We arranged to meet for lunch the next day.

The three regular daily broadcasts went well – technically that is – for several days. Then, on September 29, in Munich, Hitler, Mussolini, Chamberlain and Daladier signed their infamous agreement on the dismemberment of Czechoslovakia and the surrender of the Sudetanland to the Third Reich – announced the next day by Beneš. That day the Griffins, Beuve-Méry and the Sheeans came for the last time to give their passionate accounts of how the people were reacting. Sheean, having delivered his message, charged out of the studio.

"If at any time you need my help, please let me know," said Beuve-Méry, giving me his Paris telephone number.

The Griffins stayed another day or two and we saw a lot of each other, eating in the Vanha fish restaurant in Wenceslas Square.

The following year I managed to flee from Prague to Yugoslavia, then with the help of Beuve-Méry to France, where I joined the Czech Legion in Marseilles as a volunteer. After the collapse of France, I was evacuated with parts of the Legion to this country and arrived at Cholmondeley Park Camp. There I received an invitation from Jonathan to visit him in London. I arrived at Jonathan's flat in Westminster early in the afternoon. I answered his flood of questions. How did I fare after his departure from Prague? Did I agree, or disagree, with the politics and actions of Beneš? Could he have done other than he did? How did I manage to flee from Prague? What about the Nazi rule over my unhappy land? How did I get to France? And then he told me: "We were trying to get you out of France.." "Why? Who?" I asked. "The BBC was already interested in you...listen, would you consider the BBC's offer to join the new Czech Section as its programme organiser? We have made our enquiries..and your military people are willing to release you for this job". Without hesitation I accepted. Sure enough, a few days later I was told by my CO I was on unlimited leave from my unit... Would I report to Sir John Lawrence the next day at 10 a.m. in Broadcasting House.

After all formalities had been dealt with I went to find Jonathan, who was based at Bedford College. He showed me my office and my secretary and introduced me to Louis MacNeice, the poet and to John Ireland, the composer who was my neighbour for the months I worked there. Jonathan followed my activities with interest and was open to discussion whenever I would feel the need for it. Very soon a serious problem arose. Dr. Beneš set up a broadcasting department within his government-in-exile. The BBC was formally notified; the chief of the department would be very welcome at the weekly programme conference. There the man, not very courteously, indeed roughly, opposed all BBC plans for programmes, hardly bothering to support his views with arguments. The conference, under the chairmanship of Sir John Lawrence, was attended by Jonathan, Geoffrey Lias the representative of the Ministry of Information, myself and Beneš' man. Jonathan always supported me and so did Lias and Sir John. At that time, as we knew, Beneš had officially asked the BBC for a portion of the evening broadcasting time; his broadcasting department would provide speakers. Beneš's request was granted; it was a political matter agreed between the British government, the BBC and Beneš. The result was that this man tried hard to extend his sway over my programmes. The position could not be worse: there was a sort of Czech government, backed by the British authorities; there was the BBC constrained by this situation; there was myself, just an old broadcasting worker without any political backing. Untenable. So I resigned and returned to my army unit. Even so, Sir John and Jonathan protected the military programme that I had introduced; at least once a month, I would prepare programmes with the Czech troops and the BBC would send me their recording van.

From time to time, while visiting London on business of this sort, I would meet Jonathan, often in the Cumberland Hotel at Marble Arch, for a chat and lunch. Those meetings stopped when the Czech troops were sent to the Borders for intensive pre-invasion training. Shortly after that I was sent at my request to General Swoboda's[3] Army Corps in the USSR. I remained outside the UK for several years: at the front, and in Czechoslovakia, Canada, the USA. At the beginning of 1957 I was back in London, a former soldier, imported by the BBC from California for their Czech Section. One night at Covent Garden, I saw Jonathan, smiling and stretching out his hand. There could not have been a nicer way of inaugurating the second period of our friendship. I would come often to Jonathan's house at Markham Street in Chelsea for tea or lunch or dinner. I met Jonathan's second wife, Kathleen, whom I learned to love. What did we talk about? Politics, life, literature, arts, theatre, music, above all poetry. It was very strange, that we both, in our fifties, suddenly, without any doubt or hesitation, set our future course firmly under the stewardship of the Muse. Jonathan, I saw, had thrown himself vehemently onto a path where brushing aside all encumbrances like a regular job, he could contribute so much to English literature: his own poems and his admirable translations from French, German and above all from Portuguese. Over the years, he would give me his latest book of poetry, of translations, inscribed with warm words. At the beginning of that resolute activity, we spoke once about pressures of time. I happened to say: "Our writing first..we do not have much time left." He repeated the words, deeply moved.

Jonathan and Kathleen moved to their new house in north London. I would go there for tea, it was already difficult to hear Jonathan properly: his soft speech and my deteriorating hearing! It was a difficult time for me. I can never be sufficiently grateful to Jonathan and Kathleen for the support they gave me, for the pleasure too of listening to Jonathan reading poems, out aloud, in whispers; for his translating some of my poetry.

So it went on year by year, with gaps created by Jonathan's absence on reading and lecture tours in the USA and travels elsewhere. In his last phase Jonathan would speak softer and softer and Kathleen would repeat his words in a loud voice. So there he is, reading in his melodious voice a new poem, and allowing for frequent caesuras...which have, to my sorrow and loss, set in for good.

Editor's notes
1.   Later to become founder editor of *Le Monde*. I expect it was he who introduced Jonathan to de Gaulle when the latter needed a translator for his memoirs. According to Griffin, de Gaulle's English was much better than he ever let on in public.
2.   Later to become a well-known journalist.
3.   Later President of Czechoslovakia at the time of the Soviet invasion.

LOUIS AND ANNETTE KAUFMAN

We met Jonathan in Paris in 1949, at an evening "open house" gathering of assorted writers, musicians, poets, actors, diplomats, painters and ballet-dancers that Cecil Robson held infrequently at 75 rue Notre-Dame-des-Champs. His spacious white two storey dwelling, semi-hidden, behind a wall facing the street, enclosed an attractive garden and a neighbouring house, where painter Othon Friesz formerly lived and worked, and was then occupied by Mané-Katz (recently returned from "exile-in-New York").

No-one was formally introduced at these varied côteries. Jonathan seemed isolated in a comfortable chair near us and we introduced ourselves and enjoyed a lively un-interrupted conversation about music and theatre. We discovered we shared enthusiasm for Mozart, Wagner and Strauss operas – and various singers. As the evening drew to a close, Louis offered "May we drive you home? We've a small quatre cheveaux Renault outside." Jonathan smiled, "I live just across the street!"

Jonathan knew everyone in "le tout Paris" – the statesmen, the political figures, radio and newspaper editors and journalists, playwrights, actors, artists and musicians. We often met Jonathan at Cecil's, when we would listen for hours to great recordings, and began to occasionally dine together at small nearby bistros. We attended de Musset's *Lorenzaccio* and plays of Claudel, Garcia Lorca and Ionesco with him. Jonathan introduced us to the writing of Kazantzakis.

In fall 1949 Louis' debut was at an all-Milhaud concert, playing the Second Milhaud violin concerto with Darius Milhaud as director of l'Orchestre Nationale at the Théâtre des Champs-Elysees. We had recently found in the Library of Brussels' Conservatoire Royale the first edition (printed by Michel Le Cene in 1725) of Vivaldi's 12 Concerti: – Opus VIII – "Il Cimento dell'Armonia e Dell'Invenzione". We asked an Italian diplomat the meaning of *Cimento*, he thought it an obsolete term meaning welding or marriage. However, Jonathan had the solution – he had picked up an 18th century Italo-English lexicon at Sotheby's, stating *Cimento* (a medieval term used in jousting) should be translated as contest or conflict. So we proceeded with "The Conflict between Harmony and Invention" which became generally accepted.

Browsing at a quai bookstall, where he bought a narrative of "The Inquisition at Goa", Jonathan became fascinated by the 16th century tragedy of King Sebastian, who lost his Portuguese Empire in one ill-conceived North African battle – and whose body was never found. He became engrossed in writing a play to explore the possibility that one of the many contenders for the Portuguese throne might be King Sebastian – chastened by the military disaster to disappear until he was worthy of his lost Kingdom. He would occasionally read a section to us in Paris and once when we were together in England at his family home in Henley-on-Thames. Then he realized the subject demanded poetry and he re-cast the Trilogy into verse. We both have always considered *The Hidden King* one of the greatest dramas of our century. We have treasured all Jonathan's poetry, and translations of novels, biographies and his talent for Portuguese poetry.

Cecil greeted us one evening, delightedly, with "Jonathan has fallen in love with an English lady, and is returning to London!" This gave us the opportunity to meet the attractive Kathleen, who loved and inspired Jonathan to achieve his life's work. Her enthusiastic support and understanding encouraged his every aspiration in life. She rejoiced in the publication of *The Hidden King* and its brilliant premiere at the Edinburgh Festival.

Our long un-interrupted friendship with Jonathan gave us the opportunity to appreciate his vast culture. He was a true Renaissance gentleman; he had wide political experience and military knowledge; he was conversant with world literature and poetry; he had an intimate love and understanding of music in all forms; he was at home in all the arts and sciences, and had a great talent for poetic writing and translation.

His overwhelming modesty obscured his deep appreciation and knowledge of universal arts and human problems. Our lives were greatly enriched by our long and devoted friendship.

SIR JOHN LAWRENCE

Jonathan Griffin and I were exact contemporaries at New College Oxford. We read Mods and Greats together and went to the same lectures. We soon became friends, a friendship that lasted into its seventh decade. We shared an enthusiasm for all the arts. One of my most vivid memories of my Oxford days is of Jonathan and me passing a particularly beautiful birch tree, which then stood in New College's lovely garden, surrounded on one side by Oxford's medieval walls; he spoke of the Dolmetsches and the early music that they were then discovering.

After we went down from Oxford we were drawn together by liberal values, with a small 'l'. We lived through the agonising thirties, when the world was slowly slipping into the second world war. We were among those who saw clearly what Hitler was and we struggled in vain to make others see what we could see all too plainly. Jonathan lived in a Bloomsbury flat surrounded by original Picassos and a particularly lovely Marie Laurencin. At this time he wrote a book on the probable consequences of aerial bombardment, which turned out to be too pessimistic but we took it seriously at the time. This was Jonathan's Czech period and he brought us vivid news of that tragic country. How he must rejoice in heaven that Czechoslovakia is at last free!

In September 1939 the long awaited war was finally upon us. I am asthmatic, which barred me from military service, but in August 1939 it was clear that war could no longer be avoided. So I asked my Foreign Office cousin, Gerry Young (the late Sir George Young Bt) what I had better do. Gerry said: "There is a job at the BBC, which you would stand a good chance of getting". So I put in for it. The BBC appointed me to the post of East European Intelligence Officer, for which I had at that time next to no qualifications. I reported this to Gerry telling him that I had made no claim to any special knowledge of Eastern Europe. He replied: "Don't you see? They want to make you European Intelligence Officer but there is someone already in that job, who they want to get rid of". This duly happened and in a short space of time I found myself European Intelligence Officer.

So the Eastern Europe job fell vacant. At once I thought of Jonathan, who was genuinely knowledgeable about Eastern Europe. He put in for it and got it. From then on he and I worked in a close partnership, which we shared with our French colleague, Emile Delavenay.

When the house where my family lived had to be evacuated, I shared house with Jonathan and his first wife. This was during the blitz. We worked a shortish day at the BBC trying to get home before the shrapnel began to fall. Then we worked at our various tasks. Who now remembers that the bus shelters in the London streets were originally to protect us from falling shrapnel? I remember one day during the blitz sitting with Jonathan over a cup of coffee in the basement of Broadcasting House. He said that people in Europe were looking for a visible sign that they could put up. We were going to put this in his monthly report on Eastern Europe.

I should explain that Lord Reith, the BBC's first Director General, had mistakenly moved on to other work. Without his strong hand to guide us there was departmental warfare between the news department of the BBC and the intelligence department. The staff of the news department had been forbidden to fraternize with us. Of course some of them disobeyed their instructions. But we had one statutory right which we used to the full under the brilliant leadership of the late John Salt. We were required to make a written report once a month, and this was read with attention by the news department. I had to write an introduction as head of my section but I discussed it with Jonathan and he had a free hand to make any corrections he wanted.

During the war the BBC made a tremendous impact on European public opinion. It reached a turning point with the fall of France. Emile Delavenay told me that before the net finally closed in he had received innumerable letters from France indicating the part that German propaganda had played in the French collapse. I said: "You must write a brilliant summary of the material you have and I will report this to John Salt." Emile did just that and I wrote my usual introduction. When I reported this to John Salt, he said: "I will see that this report is on the top of every Cabinet Minister's table, the moment it appears". I never knew how he did this, but very soon the policy of the government changed. We no longer said: "We give the news. Propaganda is a dirty word." So I was made European Services Organiser and Jonathan took my place as European Intelligence Officer, a post which he filled with the greatest distinction.

As part of the new policy, section meetings were organised for every country to which we broadcast. I was chairman of the Belgian meeting. The section head was Victor de Laveleye, who had been Belgian Minister of Justice before the war. His Flemish assistant was Mr Geersens.

I missed one meeting over Christmas because I had 'flu. So I did not know what had happened. On the minutes of the meeting I noticed there was an item headed, "V Sign". "What's that?" I asked. M. De Laveleye explained: "We had been reading Griffin's report and we thought that V met the case, as it stands for Victoire in French and Vrijhed, which means freedom in Flemish." "What a brilliant idea!" I exclaimed. "Yes", said my old school chum, Cecil de Saumarez, who represented the Ministry of Information, "I thought it ought to be extended to the Dutch." "Why not much wider? Let's start with the French". I told Jonathan and he said "V" in Czech stands for "Pravda vicesi" (truth will prevail), which is the motto of the Czechs and Slovaks.

The next step was to talk to Douglas Ritchie, who soon became famous for his broadcasts under the pseudonym of Colonel Brittan. He said he would put the idea to the Free French. General de Gaulle said the Free French already had their own visual sign, the Croix de Lorraine. But people had been putting up the V sign in parts of France near the Belgian border. "You can report this as a fact". Ritchie agreed. And the V Sign was launched on its course.

Churchill took it up and the BBC established a V committee. Everyone wanted to muscle in on a successful idea and the V committee soon became too large to serve any useful purpose. But it spawned one good idea. Jonathan and I were both members of the V committee. At one of our meetings a large cigar smoking man from the Ministry of Economic Warfare, whose name I forget, suggested that in the Morse Code the sign for V was three shorts and a long. Jonathan then said at once, "That's Beethoven's Fifth Symphony". The idea of an audible V sign originated with P.T. Stevens (always called Tom Brown Stevens) who saw that dot dot dot dash was the Morse Code for V. Stevens was working at the Ministry of Economic Warfare. He was another New College man, an exact contemporary of Jonathan and me. He also read Greats and became a don at Magdalen College Oxford and was an authority on Roman history.

So we had a V that was audible as well as visible and the Fifth Symphony became the sign of victory. The BBC decided to use it as an interval signal. At first we tried it on a trumpet but that was judged, quite rightly, to be too loud for what in occupied France had to be kept quiet. So we decided to have a drum beat dot dot dot dash. I had to approve the recording. I shall never forget the drummer who came to the BBC. He could not get the idea. "But there is nothing to it. You can't make it interesting." Then suddenly a gleam of recognition came into his eyes and he drummed out the famous interval signal that went out for the rest of the war.

Soon after this there was an unhappy upheaval at the BBC over which I prefer to draw a veil. John Salt was disgracefully treated and I made myself so unpopular with the new Controller of European Services that I had to find alternative employment. I was appointed Press Attaché to the British Embassy in the Soviet Union, so my close association with Jonathan ended. But I picked up with him again when he was in effect, though not in title, Cultural Attaché to our Embassy in Paris. I went to stay with him in his delightful house on the Rive gauche, at a time when Paris was only beginning to recover from the war.

From then on Jonathan was occupied with his poetry and with translations to make ends meet. He gave me a copy of *The Hidden King* which I am ashamed to say I did not read, until a mutual friend told me that he, too, had neglected to read it until recently, but he had now done so and strongly recommended it to me. Then I read it and was full of admiration for my old friend. It will be his lasting memorial. The last time I saw Jonathan with his wife Kathleen was at our mutual friend, John Wilkins' flat. We had both aged, but he gave me a copy of his last book of poems, *Commonsense of the Senses*, in which his concern for the earth finds full expression. Since then I have prayed regularly every morning that we may be forgiven for what we have done to this planet of ours and that God will renew the face of the earth.

Editor's note
The drummer was James Blades, later Professor of tympany & percussion at the Royal Academy of Music, London, who says of this episode: "During a dark period in our national history [the drum's] defiant note carried a message in a manner worthy of the instrument's tradition." Blades also played the notes made famous by the trademark giant at the beginning of J. Arthur Rank films. (See *Percussion Instruments and their History* by James Blades, Faber & Faber 1970). Thanks to poet and drummer Anthony Barnet for drawing my attention to this information after reading John Lawrence's piece on Jonathan Griffin in *The Guardian*.

KARIN LESSING

DANCE ON, TAKE . . .
in *memoriam Jonathan Griffin*

Dance on, take
grace as beginning
word   wave

no salt-weighted
wind weighs
breaks

earth roots
in tremor
the swaying stalk

     "men
making music"

bend inwards
to expand your night-
air that you came for

breathing in deeper
and hearing

where it opens –

arches of praise   moonlit   at the edge

spring

EUGENIO LISBOA

The day is short and the work is long, says a proverb. Jonathan Griffin was, in this respect, a happy man: his work was long and his day was not short.

I had the privilege of knowing him personally as soon as I arrived in London in 1978. Before I met him he was just a name: the translator of Fernando Pessoa. A translator, we are inclined to think, is not exactly a writer; even less a man. How wrong we are. How particularly wrong I was in the case of Jonathan. He was an excellent poet and a delightful human being: a learned man, he enjoyed life, meticulously; a gifted writer and music lover, he was also the most unassuming of people, an attentive listener, a self-effacing man, a peace lover and because he was happy, a promoter of happiness.

In a world and at a time when gloom is the order of the day, Jonathan, merely by his presence, has somehow reassured us: the world might be saved if it produces more people like the author of *The Hidden King*.

During the second world war Jonathan very appropriately was in charge of raising the morale of the allies. This bent remained with him. To be with him, to do things with him, to read his poetry could transform our lives for the better.

We, Portuguese, owe him an immense debt for he translated Camões, Pessoa and many other important poets. But I, personally, was always under the distinct impression that my debt to him was of another kind: a certain form of inner peace, of strange reconciliation with the world and hopefully with myself. Only special people can produce such effects. Jonathan was one of them. They are – more and more I believe it – the true poets.

HELDER MACEDO

In 1972, when I was organizing a special number of *Modern Poetry in Translation* devoted to Portuguese poetry, I received a letter from someone whose name I thought I recognized but could not immediately place. The tone was courteous, unassuming, almost diffident. The writer had done some translations of Fernando Pessoa's poems, wondered if I would like to see them. I thought he must be one of the young poets who at that time orbited around Ted Hughes (Hughes had given the project his blessing) and felt it was my duty to encourage him. But the handwriting – an erudite spider's scrawl – belonged to another time, and the suggestion that we meet for tea did not quite correspond to the youthful tone of the letter. At all events, I was very glad not to have to undergo the lukewarm beer of a London pub and duly telephoned the number given. Why not at his house, he suggested, near Primrose Hill? I agreed.

And so I found myself, one afternoon, sitting in a room with Jonathan Griffin, a Romney, a Leslie Hurry or two, a large antique table covered with books, a Napoleonic chair covered with cats, the first edition of Faria e Sousa's Camões. And many other treasures which emerged from the casual profusion over years of a growing friendship. Some of the furniture seemed too big for the charming 'two-two-two' house, as though it had come from some ancestral palace. And indeed it had – from a country house whose baroque theatre had once been auctioned by Mr Christie to pay Lord Barrymore's debts.

Jonathan Griffin was then around 65. Tall, thin, frail-looking, incredibly vigorous. He had refused a pre-established destiny, rejecting the military career traditionally followed by his family. He was a man of deep culture and multiple talents. He could have become a professional musician; he attended Schnabel's master classes, worked with Dolmetsch, knew Nadia Boulanger and Pierre Boulez. He gave the first performance in England of Berg's piano sonata. During the second world war, he was the director of BBC European Intelligence and in the immediate post-war years served with the British Embassy in Paris in the Cultural and Press sections. He had met everyone – all the writers, painters, actors who had made Paris the intellectual Mecca of my formative years. He talked about them without exhibitionism; it would take me a moment or two to realize that the subject of one of his amusing anecdotes actually was Claudel, for example, or Jean-Louis Barrault. When he wanted to emphasize something he lowered his voice. When he was particularly pleased, he purred like a cat. Indeed, the much-loved cats of the Griffin household must have learned to purr from him, for he was a man of frequent and generous enjoyments. If an actor had managed to shine in a fairly mediocre production of some play, the entire evening would be remembered in terms of that performance. 'Wasn't it wonderful?', he would say, and we would find ourselves agreeing that it had indeed been wonderful, learning the implicit lesson that there is more pleasure to be had from praising what is good than from criticizing what is bad.

His wife, Kathleen, who also speaks the language of cats, was the perfect companion, conjuring out of the daily business of living a life blessed by the gods. Her magic touch must have owed something to her background of High Church and Theatre (the heroic days of the Old Vic), a powerful metaphysical combination that made it possible for dinner guests to find themselves participating in a discussion on the nature of evil in Macbeth between an eminent theologian and one of the most brilliant Shakespearian actors of his generation.

Jonathan Griffin's interest in Portugal went back a long way. He had known Alberto de Lacerda and Jorge de Sena, some of whose poems he translated. In 1957, the talking point of the Edinburgh Festival was his verse play *The Hidden King* based on the legend of the return of the young King Sebastian to rule Portugal again in a new age of glory. A spectacle originally designed to last six hours and to happen simultaneously on three stages, *The Hidden King* (which I did not see performed) seems to have elements of Verdi's operas, Claudel's plays and Abel Gance's films. But, above all, it epitomizes Jonathan Griffin's very special poetic diction.

His poetry is, however, only belatedly receiving critical

attention. The two large volumes of the *Collected Poems*, which he managed to put together before his death, were published in 1989 by the prestigious National Poetry Foundation of Maine. But Jonathan Griffin's translations from German, French and Portuguese were always widely praised. His translations of Fernando Pessoa introduced many English readers to the work of this major European poet and his introduction to the 'Griffin' Pessoa, published by Penguin Books, continues to be the finest study of this poet in English.

In 1986, the President of Portugal made Jonathan Griffin a knight of the Order of Saint James and, shortly afterwards, France also honoured him with the Ordre des Arts et des Lettres. The insignia of the Portuguese Order were placed on his coffin during the beautiful requiem mass sung for him at St Mary's, a church which this open-minded agnostic attended because of the marvellous quality of its music, the sober theatricality of its ritual, its true sense of religion which, on that moving occasion, effectively managed to bind together a congregation made up of people of all ages and of the most diverse religious and cultural origins, in celebration of the supreme miracle of friendship.

Editor's note
The formal tone of Helder Macedo's contribution is explained by its origin: an obituary notice – in Portuguese – first published in *Cóloquio/Letras* 113–114, Lisbon 1990.

"Y-e-e-es?" – the head a little forward, eyes round, glasses gleaming, the voice rising at least a fifth, sometimes nearer an octave, and ending with a gleeful little chuckle of shared enjoyment – that's the Jonathan I shall always remember most easily.

Enjoyment was the keynote, whether of music, or of some remote "vaut le voyage" one had at last managed to visit, or of a particularly bawdy limerick one had just picked up; but the *sharing* of it was just as important, whichever way it went, from him to you or vice versa. He loved to share his friends too, and I can hardly begin to compute the number of fascinating and amusing people, of all ages, races and sexes, that I met over the years at his and Kate's various dinner-tables. Sometimes, it's true, if one had been to a concert or a play with Jonathan, it seemed as if he was trying to redouble his own enjoyment by enjoying yours too. "Eat your own ice- cream!", one felt like telling him – but it would have been mean and pointless, because he wanted you to enjoy everything he enjoyed, and would never have understood the unworthy need that some of us have to hug delight to ourselves for a while.

In any case, so far as I was concerned Jonathan gave far more than I'm afraid he got. Perhaps with music, which was our first meeting-point, I may have been able to bring him as much enjoyment as he brought me: he loved to be alerted to new pieces, new artists, new recordings. But with a host of other things – books, paintings, buildings, landscapes – Jonathan was constantly opening my eyes and ears (taste-buds too, now that I come to think of it) to experiences I might otherwise never have had. Shared holidays in Cornwall and in France are as sharp in my mind today as when we took them 25 and more years ago – and only partly because they marked the memorable beginnings of Kate's career as a driver. It always used to astonish the pedantic map-reader in me that Jonathan, though quite incapable of telling poor Kate in time whether to turn left or right at the next junction, always seemed to have within himself some eagle's-eye view of the entire landscape that led us infallibly in the right direction. Had he been there before? If he had, it must have been long since, yet the intensity of his experience had made it indelibly part of him, and that intensity was what he communicated to his friends. One had only to share the drive down to Aldeburgh with him, a trip he had made dozens of times, to realise that his relish for Suffolk fields and churches and hedgerows never staled, and never could.

I can see him now, taking a first luxurious sniff of the east wind at Snape Maltings, or perched on the balcony at Market Cross Place sharing the early morning sun with whatever birds chose to keep him company. It was this intense appreciation of the world around him that lay behind the ecological pessimism of his later poetry and gave it its special poignancy – the knowledge that the things which gave him the most intense delight, the song or flight of birds, the air itself (for all his love of landscape, air rather than earth was his element) were in mortal danger from man's shortsightedness and greed. Jonathan once startled me by saying, over a dinner at Mustoe's, that he thought of himself as an *homme de gauche*. He probably had been before the war, and no doubt that was part of his self-image among the friends he made during the happy years he spent in Paris just after it. But by the time I knew him in the early '60s, Jonathan had, I think, lost any faith he may once have had in communal answers to social problems. He kept up with political events, it's true, and never abandoned his daily reading of *The Times* in spite of its marked swing to the right; his comments on events and personalities were informed and shrewd. But the Jonathan I knew had come to think the long-term problems of humanity insoluble; for his real life was lived at the individual level.

It was all too easy to put Jonathan down as a kind of aesthetic gourmand, and some of the professional musicians among his and my friends did just that. But anyone who was privileged to hear him talk about people – not personal relations in the abstract, which hardly interested him at all – knew that he was a wise and humane man, slow to judge, but unsparing once had had made up his mind. And that in itself gave great value to his friendship, and great weight to his criticism, however gently, even reluctantly, he might proffer it. I only realise now that he is gone how much his example, quite unconsciously, has influenced my own conception of teaching as the communication of shared enjoyment. He was fun to be with, cheerful as only a true pessimist can be. I remember him not with sadness but with deep and lasting gratitude.

PAUL OPPENHEIMER

The last time I met him was for lunch shortly before he died. He was tall and thin with naughty blue eyes and a face that looked as though it had been sharpened by being held for a long time into a hurricane. His poetry was just being published in a collected volume in Maine, and he seemed happy about that. His translations of Pessoa's peotry had just been reprinted. If anything, he was happier about that, getting someone else's work into English and out among a public that might be truly appreciative. He spoke a bit about working at the British Embassy in Paris after the war: Bertrand Russell had to be met and bundled into various black sedans for lectures he was giving and had been "nasty in a pleasant wort of way." His pasta got cold under his enthusiasm, the sort of energy that is always a sign of intelligence if not of practicality. He was interested in everyone else. There was a sea of jaunty grace in his eyes, and yet one felt an intense reliability, that he was very strong. To a younger poet aware of the consequences of choosing such a precarious type of life, this was immensely encouraging, a gift, an intimacy of surprising value. We shook hands on it.

P.K. PAIGE

OUT HERE: FLOWERING

'I have not been a tree long enough yet.'
–Jonathan Griffin

Such stern weather. Metallic. When I was a human child
my surrogate mother smiled like that –
frostily from stone eyes – no heart in it –
a withering blasted cold
that coated me with ice – I, a small tree glistening in a
    field
of glassy snow – shot
beautifully through with rainbows and somehow –
    absolute.
But spoiled. Utterly spoiled.

No wonder the blossoming has been slow,
the springs like flares, the crowding flowers
a surfeit of whipped cream. How many years have I
    stood sere
brown and unseasonable in the subliming air?
But now the melt has begun and the weather pours
over me in a pelt of petalled snow.

from: *Evening Dance of the Grey Flies*, OUP, 1981

DAVID PINNER

MUSIC
to Jonathan who embraced music and words
with equal love and fervour

Why can music reach us
When words fail us and we falter?
Perhaps because although words can teach us
And sometimes substantially alter
The thinking of our contorted lives,
Music steals deeper
And ravishes the heart's centre.

Compared to which, words,
With their pathetic, literal meanings,
Are like the inane chitterings
Of those mechanical, enamelled birds
Kept in cages by senile Emperors
At the beginnings of the know-all world.

The royal claw tightens the verbal key.
The bird's beak jerks in deference.
At times, its metal tongue burbles sense.
At others, mere bombast and mortality.
And sometimes, because of the decadence
Of an age that needs to invent talking fowl,
The clockwork feathers will only howl.

Occasionally, however,
In the world of ever-never,
The Emperor's golden birds
Exceed the wound-up limits
Of their inventors' minds.
Then the words they chime
Achieve music of a kind
That for a little time,
Reminds us of real music,
Which sings eternal
In the haunted temple
Of the mind.

For though music may teach us
Nothing
But how to dance and sing,
It can always reach,
And is always true,
And will save us
When words fail us,
As they do
Most of the time.

LAWRENCE PITKETHLY

I met him at a poetry reading in my Queensgate Terrace student flat. That afternoon my room-mate and I had borrowed twenty collapsible chairs from St. Mary Abbots. We placed candles on the improvised bookcases mounted with bricks, and two bottles of Nuits St. Georges and a vase of carnations on the square oak table by the window next to which the poets would sit. On the opposite wall was a large Slade canvas of an English picnic in the twenties done in the neo-realist style – the room's only aesthetic flourish. Throughout the reading I was aware of the tall, balding, bespectacled gentleman who reminded me of one of my University College professors. He was the oldest person there, and his presence helped to distinguish what would otherwise have seemed a college soirée. What impressed me immediately was the quality of his concentration; he was a listener, delighted to have been asked to attend, and he took everything in, responding gratefully to each poem that he liked with obvious pleasure, and occasionally emitting a discernible, and slightly decorous, "mmmm" at the end when some image or line had impressed him. Afterwards he introduced himself to me. "And of course *you're* a poet," he said in a muted voice, so soft and measured I had to strain to hear him above the volume of conversation. And after a bit, "Well you simply must come to dinner." A summons which I accepted with alacrity. It was February 7th, 1970 and I was to know Jonathan Griffin for twenty years.

Already the will to poetry in him had reached Nietzschean proportions. He had started slowly, aware of his gifts and surer of his subject, but hesitant to tackle reality head on. And as happens with genuine artists in these conditions he had taken good care of himself, searching out the company of musicians, painters, writers and those with some breath for beauty and the arts in order to make his poetic will more muscular. Even the public identities that he had assumed as a young man, in journalism, in war-time broadcasting, as a cultural attaché in Paris after the war, helped to nurse the fledgling artist – they took

75

care of his need for experience – and to assess his own priorities. His much admired work as a translator played a not dissimilar role, acting as a bridge to his poetic territory. By the time I knew him, in his early sixties, he had reached the seedtime of his powers, and was using his masterly exegesis of the Portuguese poet, Fernando Pessoa, to coax his own work onto the page. The hands belonged to Pessoa's personae, but the voice was that of Jonathan. I would listen to it for hours at Sharpleshall street, first one poem and then another that he had finished that morning or that week, and after each one he would look up shyly, hesitant to ask for approbation, but relishing it when it was offered. And while I was discovering Pessoa, I was also coming under the spell of Griffin, hearing the spill of words in fresh arrangements, their oddly pleasing turns and juxtapositions, and absorbing their new rhythms.

He told me at our first meeting that he had found his subject – over-population. "It would be a shame," he said, "if man destroys himself before discovering himself." And the alliteration helped to make the point. In his own poetry he rarely strayed far from the theme of man's inhumanity to the planet of which he is only the custodian. In this sense, Griffin is surely earth's greatest poetic defender in England since Hopkins, for whom the dearest freshness also lived deep down in things. There were other affinities Jonathan shared with the Jesuit, not the least of which was a kinship of poetic spirit, an appetite for cramming thoughts and ideas into terse word boxes, whole rows of them, so placed that you never believed sometimes that the poet could manage the sentence, until he did and a new beauty was born. Jonathan spoke about Hopkins often, and of the letters to Robert Bridges and to Richard Watson Dixon, which were essential texts in his poetic education. But unlike Hopkins, Jonathan was not plagued by the martyr spirit, not obligated to any higher power than to his own muse, and to the reverence he felt for the divine afflatus of creation in all its forms, on the earth, in the skies and in the minds of men and women.

I knew him on several continents. I recall a cherry tree on the road to Sospel in the south of France that Jonathan noticed as we drove up into the *arrière-pays*, a thing of

Japanese delicacy, in full flower, dominating the sur-
rounding landscape, a condition which only lasted in nature for the briefest of periods – when I drove back a few
days later it was gone. I associate that tree with Jonathan
because had I not been with him I would not have seen
it, and the tree's refinement has always reminded me too
of Jonathan's classically English, gentlemanly sensibility.
Having him as companion in the Midi completed the aesthetic experience. What better place to discuss poetry and
art than in the village where Yeats had been buried,
where Gide spent his winters, where the olive tree was
over one thousand years old, and where yellow jasmine
whitened in the spring. We went to see a Giacometti
retrospective at the Fondation Maeght and marvelled at
the simplicity of the form, the elongated faces and shapes,
the twisted figures which hauntingly dramatized a narrative that seemed to have taken place in the years before
the drawings, paintings or sculptures were executed: a
story in which the world was flattened and re-built, in
which humanity was battered to pieces but managed to
endure in all of its fragmented, frightened beauty. We
spent an afternoon at the Picasso museum in Antibes, that
small pagan compound, filled with horns and pipes, with
satyrs, centaurs and goats. Through an open window the
blue silk of the Mediterranean rustled in the lightest of
breezes. This was one of the shrines of modern art, another was the Matisse chapel at Vence which we also
visited, and it was easy to feel that art could flourish given
such propitious circumstances. But it is not external conditions that create the artist. "Poetry," said my companion
over dinner that night, "begins when the internal develop-
ment is complete." And he proceeded to talk about how
he became a poet, how at first he had wanted to be a
musician and studied with Schnabel, but he wasn't good
enough. Then poetry took over. I tried to question him
about his biography, and why there was so little of it in
his work. But it was precisely on this subject that he had
the most categorical opinions. Like Eliot, he tended to believe that the greatest artists are the most concealed.
"Don't expect to find me in my poems," he says in 'Not
Sins and Glosses', "my pure joys yes/ hard-won barely
held/ faith   yes   not sins and glosses   The contrast/

between my art and my life is my pride . . . . In my art
I evade my evasions/ I go away and rise above myself".

In America he shed several skins, some of the protec-
tive Englishness, and the self-effacing wrap of the diplomat who sometimes had to be all things to all people,
when he really wanted to be much more opinionated and
take sides. I remember quoting to him Gide's view of
Rome, that he did not like it because he did not find himself very interesting there. Jonathan liked America because
it re-assured him that he was as interesting as he knew
himself to be, a sentiment reciprocated by many of the
Americans he encountered. He visited me twice in Am-
herst in the mid-seventies to read at Hampshire College
and both times got a terrific reception, especially when he
read his translation of Pessoa's "I've got a terrible cold."
He was caught up in the American energy, surrounded by
students, excited by the furious talk about poetry and life
which was in the air, enlivened by being on the same
continent that brought forth poets he revered like George
Oppen. He seemed to me, not a different person, but
more conspicuously, more actively, the poet, correspondent in the modern world, always on the look-out for a
good story, as, for instance, when we rounded a road-
bend in Vermont, and he noticed a sign: DEAF CHILD AT
PLAY. That tiny word gem Jonathan re-printed as a poem
in *In Time Of Crowding*.

I was always grateful to spend time in his company as
his spiritual intensity invariably had a purifying effect on
me. It was like listening to an extraordinary piece of
music or being in the presence of a painting that domi-
nated the room by the fact of its simply being there. I
have no idea if Jonathan was always so accomplished, if
he was naturally so spiritually refined, or if the spiritual
achievements in his life were on a par with those in his
poetry, that is to say that he worked hard at being such
an inspired and illuminating human being. But I have the
idea that much application was involved, and probably at
a considerable cost. Those of us who met him later in his
life got all the benefits. He was ready to pour out the
grace of his personality into our eager mouths. Disappointed by the meagreness of the aesthetic menu, by the
diffidence, banality, incompleteness we saw around us,

Jonathan struck us as an incredibly wholesome aesthetic treat, and we tried to appreciate him as he deserved to be appreciated.

He and his dear wife Kathy saw me through the deaths of both my parents and became a surrogate family in London. The first was of my father in May, 1970, and shortly afterwards Jonathan and I walked the beach at Aldeburgh and listened to the suck and shovel of the waves on the sand, held pebbles to the sun, felt the sky peel the shore. Deep excavations of words were beginning in me, images rising like spirits from the freshly dug earth, which I associate with that walk, and Jonathan's imposing figure in a heavy raincoat. Ten years later, when my mother died, I stayed at Sharpleshall Street for a few days. Jonathan played Fauré's *Requiem*, and Kathleen Ferrier's rendition of Brahms' *Alto Rhapsody* on the record player. We went to see Pisarro at the Royal Academy, and each picture seemed born of an act of love. I was back in the nineteenth century, in the childhood of my grandparents – in rural Ireland or France it didn't matter – the windows were wiped clean, and by a marvellously, empathetic process I was granted access to my mother's world.

Jonathan seemed to understand what I was experiencing and was endlessly patient and thoughtful. I wondered then, as I do now, how he managed to maintain such constancy, for once he gave his attention he never seemed to be distracted. He had eyes that fixed, nested, fastened, concentrated, lingered. Once inside the range of his look a friend knew that he or she was being perceived, that Jonathan was listening. And this lasted way beyond the point at which any conversation actually ended. I have known so many eyes since that turned away quickly when the meeting was over, the moment gone. Jonathan gave each encounter time to play, and I would look back after saying goodbye and always see him, as I do now, right hand half raised in a mock farewell, his way of saying I'm sure that no separation between friends is ever final because so much that is blessed has been shared.

NEVILLE PRICE

Kate and I started attending St Mary's Bourne Street about the same time. It was very early in our relationship that she asked me to attend a dinner party at her house where I was to meet her husband Jonathan. From our first meeting we got on very well indeed, and when he discovered that I was a librarian with a theatrical past of dance and drama his interest knew no bounds. It was as if we had known each other for a long time. This meeting was to lay a foundation for later discussions on art, music and theatre for which he had an insatiable appetite and of which he had a vast knowledge. Several times I would meet him at a concert, or opera, in the company of Kate or Julia Farrer, and the next day we would have a little chat on the telephone about the work.

The dinner parties at their house were memorable – actors, writers, painters, clergy, academics, were among the people they used to entertain. These functions always included fine wines, and one of my treasured memories is of Jonathan sitting at the head of the table supervising the wine while conversation, which was sharp but casual, continued through the delicious courses prepared by Kate – one remembers her fruit salad with relish. Jonathan always had a sparkle in his eye as if he were waiting to deliver a trump line.

Did you know that Jonathan danced with Serge Lifar? I always asked him to repeat this story which he told with such dry humour and wit that it made me fall about with laughter: as a young man working in the British Embassy in postwar Paris, Jonathan attended several balls and receptions. At one such party, which was attended by *le tout Paris*, every one was dancing in a carnival atmosphere and Jonathan found himself facing the great ballet dancer. Serge caught hold of him and spun him around like a top. This unexpected balletic turn landed Jonathan on a wall of dancing beauties, where he collapsed quite exhausted!

Not only on birthdays and at Christmas but also on other occasions Jonathan would squeeze a little book into my hand *apropos* some chat we'd had. On one such occasion he gave me a little book of the Portuguese poet Fernando Pessoa selected and translated by himself. He had recently been 'knighted' by the Portuguese for his contribution to Portuguese literature.

Jonathan was generous and thoughtful. He loved people and enjoyed having them around him. He had an enquiring mind and an enthusiasm for the finer things in life. Always immaculately dressed in tweeds, and in one of those beautifully knitted waistcoats designed by Kate, he epitomised a passing generation of sartorial elegance.

I shall miss our chats, I shall miss the first hand accounts of his annual visits to the Aldeburgh Festival told with such excitement and exuberance. I shall miss the wit, the charm, the soft-spoken voice. I shall remember Jonathan with love and affection.

KATHLEEN RAINE

When I think of Jonathan Griffin it is not any one of his many distinctions and achievements that comes to mind but the special atmosphere he, and his second wife, Kathleen, created together in their hospitable house. There, a rich deposit of "things new and old" was the expression of Jonathan's lifetime – of many lifetimes – from the heirlooms and family portraits recalling his descent from Louis Napoleon (whose illegitimate daughter had married his maternal grandfather) – books old and new; the privileged cats; the good wine and Kathleen's wonderful cooking; the flowing conversation among friends from all fields of the arts – music, theatre, writing, and the Church. Jonathan, ever courteous, was a quietly impassioned man, for whom the practice and transmission of all the arts of civilisation mattered above all else – and he had tried his hand at many of them with professional success. To his friends he dispensed "the bread of sweet thought and the wine of delight", bringing together young and old, the famous and the untried. He was positive and encouraging in his appreciation of any work that was authentic, however modest, but always in the context of the high and enduring standards.

As a young man he had hoped to become a concert pianist, and known Schnabel, but as he did not quite reach Schnabel's standard he gave up that intention altogether. Music remained his enduring love, and from their flat in Aldeburgh the Griffins participated in the golden age of the great music of Benjamin Britten and Peter Pears. In the theatre his great love was Shakespeare.

Until the outbreak of the Second World War he had devoted himself to journalism – for a time as the correspondent in Prague to the New York *Nation* but the war saw him as Director of BBC European Intelligence in Bush House, with a diverse team of men and women brilliantly gifted in other spheres – Simone Weil, Rafael Nadal, Miron Grindea among them. After the war he was appointed Second Secretary at the British Embassy in Paris – virtually Cultural Attaché – where he knew all the painters and writers. There was always in the Griffins' house something of the magic of the theatre; Jonathan translated the memoirs of his friend Jean-Louis Barrault and Claudel's *Partage de Midi*. His own magnum opus was a six-hour play *The Hidden King*, about Sebastian of Portugal – a succès d'estime performed at the Edinburgh Festival in 1957 with Robert Speaight, Michael MacLiammoir and Robert Eddison. His supremely good translations of the poems of Fernando Pessoa were recognised by the Portuguese Government (in 1986) with the Order of St. James of the Sword, an honour which gave him great pleasure. His culture was essentially and profoundly European – he was also a Chevalier de l'Ordre des Arts et des Lettres – as English culture among the educated classes once was, but has, regrettably, increasingly ceased to be.

As a diplomat and public servant he was a professional; son of a military family he wrote on military affairs, and his views on defence became the official policy of the pre-war Liberal party. Party politics as such had little interest for him; his commitment was rather, as always with "the politics of the unpolitical", to politics in Plato's sense, as a moral issue. Like many of his class and background at that time, he had left-wing sympathies. In his later years he leaned rather to Green issues; his concern for the future of humankind and of the planet, though too well-informed to be sentimental, was unswerving.

Jonathan Griffin's commitment to fundamental values and the arts was a total way of being; he was among those by whom civilisation is tended and created, celebrated and transmitted. This was the work to which he so industriously, lovingly, and tirelessly devoted himself; whatever he achieved was done to perfection, and for the work's sake. Great European as he was America appreciated him as a poet, more than his own country and his *Collected Poems* were published (in two volumes) late in 1989, by the University of Maine. We are proud to have published in *Temenos* translations of poems by Pessoa, and by Jean Mambrino, and a group of his own poems, at once, like himself, refined and impassioned.

Jonathan's friends loved to be in the company of a man who himself embodied, and expected of others, a certain indefinable standard – those old values which are the ground of every civilisation, beauty, truth and goodness.

Unlike his wife, he was not a committed Christian, but he had about him a certain presence of the older, classical virtues of Temperance, Fortitude, Prudence and Magnaminity, underlying the ways of his house. It's not, finally what people do, or have achieved, but what they are, that we love.

Editor's note

The formal tone of Kathleen Raine's contribution is explained by its origin: an obituary notice in *The Tablet* (10/2/1990), though only about a third of this complete text was used.

CARL RAKOSI

ARTISANS
For Jonathan Griffin
Poet, Gentleman, Friend

In the night
                    the little
cricket chirps
                    and capers.
Is he rejoicing?
                    or asking,
"Whose grave
                    is this?"
Ah yes, Who.
                    All Who's
(the voices,
                    old as earth).
Where is
                    the modern who,
the thinker,
                    the Wittgenstein?
In a midsummer
                    night's dream
with Robin Starveling
                    the tailor
and his friends,
                    a bellows –
mender & a weaver
                    who do not
know their Bottom
                    from an ass.

85

MANUEL ROSENTHAL

September 1944, Paris, just liberated from German Occupation: the French National Orchestra: it was my first appearance as a conductor since September 1939. Following the concert, among the people rushing back stage to greet me, was a tall, slim, young-looking man: "I am Jonathan Griffin, Press Attaché at the British Embassy."

From that moment on, for many many years, we saw a lot of each other. Lunches, dinners (in restaurants or at home), visits to museums, exhibitions, castles, scenery. We enjoyed exchanging opinions, ideas, whether we were in agreement or not; we seldom stopped expressing our knowledge and feelings about each other's country. Music, painting, politics, theatre, cinema, everything was a pretext to enrich the time we enjoyed spending together.

Among many discoveries I owe to Jonathan was the great – still unknown at that time – Portuguese poet Fernando Pessoa whom he was translating. Also his own drama, *The Hidden King*, which he read so movingly. It is a tragedy as important and as new as the works of Claudel.

Griffin's approach to religion was always full of original ideas, especially regarding some of our best Jesuits.

I cannot end this short and awkward homage without paying my respects and most affectionate condolences to Kathleen, Jonathan's wife. Attentive, discreet, witty, charming and a perfect hostess, she was the priceless companion of a great mind, a great man of this world, Jonathan Griffin.

DEE SEPTEMBER

SAGE EYE
for Jonathan, in memory

your eyes
golden rays of light
a clear blue ocean
floats across my mind

call me to listen and feel
the sound of words
as they tumble and fall
from your being

like cherry blossoms
glacial rock slides
the hiss of waves
sharp steel blades

poems your eyes give me
to carry as precious gifts
into the long day's journey
of my life

SEBASTIAN SHAW

I have memories of post-prandial talks with Jonathan during country walks or in front of winter fires. As he warmed to his subject the words were there all right but their intensity carried with it an increasing inaudibility so that the ends of his sentences seemed to be whispered. Yet one always got the gist. We were much of an age and he felt very strongly that though many poets were at their best when young, Auden for instance, the reverse was also true. Yeats for example. And this was certainly true of Jonathan. His poems drew on experience without losing spontaneity and freshness. Throughout his last years his poems flowed from him uninterruptedly, always potent, surprising with their beautiful intensity.

I first met Jonathan in Edinburgh while we were rehearsing his big and ambitious verse play, *The Hidden King*, for its Festival production. It had been published in book form prior to production and was heralded in a glowing introduction by the late J.C. Trewin who was then the famous drama critic of the Birmingham Post. Unfortunately most of his fellow critics disagreed with him after the première. Their judgement differed from that of the Festival Committee, the distinguished cast, many members of the public who sent supportive letters – all of whom passionately believed in the play's imaginative breadth and poetic splendours. So it was decided to hold a grand post-mortem to which all the critics were invited, members of the public, the Committee, with Lady Rosebery in the chair, the cast and last but by no means least, the author. Though Jonathan must have been deeply disappointed by his play's critical reception, I remember his saying, "They are entitled to their opinion of course, but they are wrong". Jonathan was not the first playwright to face such a barrage so it was far from wishful thinking to suppose all the critics (except one) might be wrong again. It was during this meeting when many had their say that an old man held forth so interminably and irrelevantly that Lady Rosebery appealed to the ever witty Irish actor Michael MacLiammoir to try and stop him. Michael was quite equal to this challenge. He interrupted the old man with: "I know his sort, he's the death and soul of the party". With that touch of humour Michael not only shut up the old man but also eased the tension generated by the critics' speeches of self-justification and the spirited replies of Jonathan's supporters. It was I think typical of Jonathan that he should welcome this touch of humour into these over-solemn proceedings. He told me two or three years after that he met a lady who said how delighted she was to meet him. She had never forgotten reading about his famous *The Hidden King*. The papers were full of it! "So you see Sebastian, those critics demonstrated yet again that all publicity is good publicity".

Jonathan's interest in all the arts was insatiable, particularly music. But behind all his work and indeed all his life he was in love with religion without being himself religious. To believe or not to believe? Who knows? Perhaps now he does.

Post-script by Joan Ingpen-Shaw
I remember Jonathan for his love of music, his open- mindedness about anything new and his almost puckish sense of humour. He was I suppose what is called an intellectual, with a gift of total recall of everything he had ever seen or heard, but I never felt that he was condescending to the lower level which I inhabit.

MATTHEW SWEENEY

THE KNOWING BIRDS
For Jonathan Griffin

A gull laughed at me,
laughed three times and flew on,
and the smell of dried blood
rose from the green
and followed me on the wind.
There was no escape
in the sandstone, no caves
to hide in, and the sea
was stormy, the beach boat-free.
I caught a magpie
with the side of my eye, heading
towards the house
where a family of swifts
sat on the wires
outside my window, and saw
right through me
day after day, and the baby
flew in once, and turned
in the trapped air
above me, then flew back out.
Why would it stay there?

FRANK THORNTON

"Birds of a feather flock together." This proverb is now unpopular with our political leaders who tell us we are living in a classless multi-racial society and had better enjoy it. In the real world that the rest of us occupy the old saw still seems to be widely applicable. A Masai warrior and a Wall Street banker, thrown together for a weekend, might find it difficult to exult in each other's company much past breakfast time on Saturday. An expert in Sumerian pottery is unlikely to seek out a lager lout for a pleasant evening's social intercourse.

The son of a bank clerk, leaving school at sixteen, an incompetent insurance clerk for two years, then becoming an actor, would hardly expect to strike up a friendship with a man about fifteen years his senior, of aristocratic background, university education, a career in diplomacy, and a poet. But the poet happened to write a play *The Hidden King*, in which the actor was among the "wines and spirits," i.e. a very minor player with, if any, very small billing right at the bottom of the poster.

That was thirty four years ago, since when my wife and I have enjoyed many happy and interesting hours in the company of Jonathan and Kate. I always left these meetings with the delighted feeling that yet again Jonathan had failed to notice that I was vastly his intellectual inferior. This blind spot in Jonathan's perceptions had its uses. Faced, for instance, with some of the more obscure passages in a Shakespeare play, I could consult Jonathan about them, comfortable in the knowledge that it would not occur to him for one moment that I might be totally incapable of understanding them anyway, whatever he might say about them. We faced each other on an apparent basis of intellectual equality.

We like to think we know our friends but be warned! In 1976 Jonathan was in Manchester for the opening of his adaptation of Kleist's *The Prince of Homburg* at the Royal Exchange Theatre and agreed to spend the weekend at the little country hotel where I lived while performing at Blackpool in a stage version of a T.V. situation comedy. (Jonathan never owned a television set.) On the Sunday he out-walked me in the Trough of Bowland (did I say fifteen years my senior?). But that was after a Saturday I had looked forward to with some trepidation. I tried every way I could think of to prevent my friend attending the evening's performance, assuring him that it was very much not his cup of tea. I failed.

He arrived just before the matinée and announced that he would spend the afternoon exploring Blackpool. Jonathan Griffin exploring Blackpool! A translator of Portuguese poetry in the land of candy-floss and whelks! One accepted in General de Gaulle's circle rubbing shoulders with girls in "Kiss-me-quick" hats! Where could he be more out of place?

Once again Jonathan failed to live up to my expectations. He arrived back in my dressing-room for a between-shows shortbread and a cup of tea, his sparse grey hair ruffled by the coastal breeze, his eyes shining behind his round steel spectacles and gave me an enthralling account of all the mysteries and delights he had encountered. He could hardly have enjoyed himself more. And he even enjoyed the play! That was Jonathan Griffin for you.

Life of a Poet

On the eightieth birthday of a poet, it seems fitting to raise the question with which each soul comes into the world: *What was I born for?* We answer ourselves truly and falsely many times a day. Children raise the question when they grasp a handful of raw earth and taste it, or when they meet a stranger's fatuous smile with their own shining, unbeholden one. Cynics distract themselves with various forms of dissipation, including despair, from the fear that there may be no answer. Tyrants resolve the question by imposing a 'solution' upon those in their power. Lovers and saints believe that their answer has been revealed, for love, in all its forms, is the feeling, 'I was born for this'.

Poets have a more difficult and in a way more privileged relation to fate, for which each new poem is a little paradigm. Language constantly chastens the poet by reminding him that all intentions bend when you express them. To live is as to write: to remain scrupulously, passionately, furiously, humbly attentive. That, I think, is what makes poetry useful. For when I grapple with the question of what I was born for, the common formulas — 'the look heres!' — are of much less value than the uniquely concrete examples: 'I have looked here'. A poem is an upturned stone.

Jonathan Griffin has reached eighty. When you listen to a piece of music with him, or walk along a path you thought familiar, or when he takes you into an old church, or reads to you from a new book, you become aware that his capacity for attentiveness — passion, fury, humility and precision — has grown stronger with the years, not weaker. If his poetry 'rings true and jars the strict to ecstasy and haunts strangers', it is because he has permitted it, and himself, to become more, not less, unsure. That seems to be the hallmark of the most powerful 'late fruit work'.

The gift Jonathan offers with so much courage, particularly to those of us who are younger and further behind, is not that benevolent reassurance so often taken for wisdom. It is solidarity in our unknowingness.

> 'Love   blind
>   so'

Love just so.

JUDITH THURMAN, May 18, 1986

Extra-special MenCard 96 published by The Menard Press in 1986 to mark the 80th birthday of Jonathan Griffin on May 14

DANIEL WEISSBORT

I see him, courtly impish, or impishly courtly. I see him, not so long ago, at the Poetry Society. Or is it, rather, the reception at the Voice Box for the "Child of Europe" poetry readings? Or it's earlier, at the Tavola Calda in High Holborn where we'd regularly meet, on my periodic returns to London, over the last fifteen years or so. And before that there was a charabanc-load of us, in Ipswich, for the first night of Jonathan's splendid translation of Claudel's *Partage de Midi*, starring the then unknown Ben Kingsley – Jonathan, almost paroxysmically delighted, hosting the whole affair in his quintessentially theatrical style! He enjoyed himself more self-indulgently and yet less egotistically than anyone I knew...

He got frailer (or should one say his frailness grew frail, since there seemed always to be a kind of genteel frailness about him, at least in the twenty odd years that I knew him?). Yet he didn't really change, even if he insisted he was changing, losing his memory, becoming – a wry smile! – senile. Though elated by his victory over cancer, increasingly he talked of his physical decline. Humorously, slightly contentiously. Not exactly angrily, not exactly apologetically either. And I'd indulge him and chide him a little, as one does in such circumstances. His memory, it is true, was unsure, though never as far as I could tell, crucially. It was more like being in the "gods", with Jonathan smiling down on himself playing Polonius or some other wise, foolish or forgetful old man! And I'm happy to say he never forgot me, or if he did – even that would not really have been crucial – he disguised it consumately. Of course, I'd have co-operated too, wanting to be taken in! But then one did – that is, one did co-operate with Jonathan, since to do so was pleasurable, you might even say empowering, as when a master fills you with a sense of your own worth.

That smile, then the stooped, courtly greeting – the slight aura of wickedness? So, no, he didn't grow old exactly. The body, yes, with him apologizing and complaining a little, in his well-bred manner. Not panicking, but with a kind of disbelief, or as if this were one part which, despite its rich potential, he was, after all, not too sure he relished.

What has all this to do with Jonathan, the translator? (More, perhaps, than meets the eye, though I shall steer clear of psychological claptrap!) Because, after all, how else did I know him? A master translator. He gave me my due, whatever that may have been. And every now and then, we engaged professionally. It was like a kind of dance, with me as the pupil and him as the instructor, an ideal instructor who always left me feeling enriched, flattered. But, alas my own memory – a good deal worse than his was, even in these latter years – does not return to me what he said about translation. Did I simply absorb it, translate it! I wrote to him, when I was assembling a collection of papers on the translation of poetry, but he didn't answer. No doubt it was too late for that sort of thing. More regrettably, perhaps, at a time when Jonathan was regularly contributing to *Modern Poetry in Translation*, a magazine I edited for many years, I did not take the opportunity of teasing from him some theoretical commentary. Somehow I thought it would be indelicate to ask! I'd have hoped to elicit more than the belletristic response which, I dare say, would have been his first, since Jonathan would have wrongly felt he would bore our readers. I'd have hoped to persuade him that. Would our discourse have permitted this? On second thoughts, I think perhaps it would. Pity!...

Tony Rudolf kindly suggested I might wish to contribute a poem to this collective tribute. Perhaps one would come. It didn't. But I am reminded that it was really Tony who mediated my relationship with Jonathan. Tony looked after him, literally, but also by according him – and making sure he was accorded – the esteem, the appreciation as a writer (i.e. not "just" a translator), that was his due, but which there is no guarantee – the literary world being no better than it should be – he would have received. Tony published his poetry as well as other works by him. But, above all, he appreciated and insisted on Jonathan's uniqueness, or should we say his dedication? Maybe we should, but then Jonathan was a prince, and princes are not exactly dedicated: it is more a question of *noblesse oblige*.

Which reminds me of a delightful occasion – this time it *is* the Poetry Society – when an unsuspecting Jonathan received from the Portuguese Cultural Attaché an honorary knighthood, for his services to Portuguese literature (his wonderful translations of Pessoa). He loved it, of course, seemed genuinely surprised. Was he? Perhaps such public acknowledgement could still surprise him. At any rate, I am convinced that it was rather that he *contrived* to be so! His breeding helped, of course. But the delight flowed over. Delight – and amusement? I wonder...

I knew so little about him, though perhaps I knew him as well as it was appropriate for me to know him; at least I didn't overstep the mark. A master then, with that helplessness of the master. As though, actually, his true life was lived on some other plane, even if he was perfectly content to share ours too.

Is this an exaggeration! I can hear Jonathan chuckle. Yes, that chuckle, the appreciative, attentive murmur too; the head nodding, cheeks drawn in, lips pursed... Suddenly, I miss him.

SUSANNAH YORK

For Jonathan, without whom

Jonathan as long as I knew him bore a shining countenance; I'm sure he always did for in that aged face nothing was more discernible than the small boy, merry, kind, naughty, bursting with secrets and questions and life.

I'd discovered Claudel's *Partage de Midi* and determined I must play Ysé. No, no-one knew of an English version. I began to make heavy weather of the first pages of a first attempt, but then, yes! I heard; the poet Jonathan Griffin had translated it some years ago, Ben Kingsley had played Mesa, there'd been a succès d'estime at Norwich ... I tracked Jonathan down.

By this time I'd discovered and read Claudel's two later versions of the play. The original – from which my enthusiasm had stemmed – was more poem than play, a glorious metaphysical piece rich in characterisation and *vie intérieure* but untheatrical; and Jonathan's translation of that 1905 version had those same qualities, but lacked the vocal rhythms of the French. On better acquaintance it was clear to me why Barrault whilst twisting Claudel's arm in the early forties for the rights to the play, had insisted on extensive rewriting. Claudel himself wanted them in this his most personal work, and the first 'version pour la scène' contained much new material to make it stage-worthy, even coarse in its theatricality. Evidently Claudel and Barrault soon thought so too, for when the play was revived some five years later, there was a newly cut and reshaped second 'version pour la scène', but to my mind (and Jonathan's too, when he read them) still some of the fineness of the original was gone.

Sage, or elf, was he? Both of course, but sage is what I knew of that first meeting, sage, poet, diplomat, linguist: and those are whom I asked, not very hopefully, if they would consider working with me from scratch on not just a new translation, but a new version. 'Structure comes naturally to actors,' David Hare told me once: I felt essential to the reassembly. There's nothing like a plethora of indifferent scripts, either, for teaching you sayability ... I felt essential to the translation too. Perhaps between us, headlong actor, faithful poet, we could, whilst being true to Claudel, muster the inspiration needed to bring this very French piece to the English stage? To my everlasting enchantment Jonathan agreed.

I never found out whether he had collaborated in this way before, it seemed we were making up the way to work; at any rate I hadn't, and should it happen again I know I can't expect such joy. For three glorious summer months on and off we worked. At each day's end we'd repair with our 'devoir', the next pages to be individually prepared, and three or four mornings a week I would dash over to Primrose Hill (the sun seemed always to be shining), listen for the shuffling of Jonathan's sandals on the parquet. Spectacles skew-whiff, pencil 'twixt ear and finger, this etiolated pixie would sit me down at the dining-room table where he'd already been working and together we'd prise out, tease out, extract meaning, bend into English rhythms this dense and wondrous prose. He'd have no truck from me over our disparity in age, experience, status, exacting no quarter and giving none: and while again and again we'd agree on the happiest rendering of a word, a thought, a passage, just as often we didn't, Jonathan always fighting for the most exact translation, I for what, tried out on my tongue, could be said. Remarkable powers of persuasion would swing into play...

Golden hours. We worked joyfully, relentlessly, gasping for air after three or four hours, gulping down Kate's sandwiches sometimes, but mostly repairing to the pub where sitting in a stained-glass glow, we'd devour fish and chips or huge cheese-and-tomato rolls, as well as a good glassful each of wine as golden; talk the play, talk Claudel, Jonathan's diplomatic work in Paris, an opera he'd just seen, the jobs I was between, Aldeburgh, politics, Jesuitry, poetry, theatre, family, life ... and rush back to work at the dining-room table until the preparing sounds of Kate and our stomachs and the disappearing sunlight told us it was teatime and after. And one day we finished. Apparently we'd finished.

Laid down our pencils by the sheaves of paper scribbled and rescribbled over, on the dining-room table, and tiptoed away for tea, our last tea, Kate pouring, and those wonderful macaroons from Marks and Spencer and the chocolate cake: solemnly, sadly, chortling with achievement amongst the portraits in the sitting-room while the outrageously fat tabby purred. We knew it wasn't the end though; I was to take home the wads of paper, type them up, and next week we'd have a grand reading in my sitting-room. A grand reading of two. I'd read, Jonathan would listen. And after that the National and the RSC and Jonathan Miller at the Old Vic, the English-speaking world would be fighting for a chance to mount it, Kingsley and McKellen and Holm to play Mesa, Blakely and Jacobi and Gambon, Amalric...

But that's not what happened. Reading it aloud days later, I tripped and stumbled frequently, unaccustomedly; and realised in some despair that we were still very far from a final draft, though Jonathan professed himself pleased. The differences of our viewpoints sprang (perhaps?), from the fact that he 'saw' the text on the page, approved its literary authenticity: I said it, kept saying it, large chunks, and imaginatively hearing it both in my mouth and others' ... and what so often *looked* real and true hardly sounded so, Claudel's passion dressed in English weights ...

I put it away.

Over a year later I was touring in 'The Glass Menagerie'. Once you feel you have your character and her story in the bone – and three weeks after opening I felt that with Amanda – you suddenly feel released, stimulated in fact to take on others, another, their story. I re-read our translation. It didn't feel performable.

Starting again from scratch from the three French versions, with my so much augmented knowledge and understanding, was hardly even a decision. I left the translation in London, and easily unlearning the adopted metre in Swansea and Buxton and Norwich did just that for two or three pages, five or six ... Three and a half weeks later the revised text and a new translation were done. It was a very different thing.

For weeks, for months I procrastinated about ringing Jonathan. Would he feel hurt, offended, used? How would he feel about his name there? How did I?

Eventually I rang him, and sent it, and waited ...

He was speedy, and absolutely grand of course. 'Well, You've taken my breath away. It's marvellous. It's hardly the same thing. Marvellous though. All the same ...' Winded, he sounded, but giggling and full of the same glorious enthusiasm for the play, and no, there'd been no travesty. 'But if I might make one or two observations ...' and of course he was wonderfully pertinent over a Kate tea.

Later, through Tony, I learned that delicacy forbade him to suggest his name be taken off the translation, lest I suspect some private reservations. But were the suggestion to come from *me* ...

When it is played it will be dedicated 'To Jonathan without whom.'

Editor's post-script

Susannah York's translation of *Partage de Midi, Noonbreak*, was presented at the French Institute from November 19 till December 8, 1991 and then in the Green Room at the Manchester Royal Exchange Theatre. It was directed by Eloi Recoing, with Susannah York as Ysé, Michael Thomas as Mesa, Tim Woodward and Sam Cox as Amalric and De Ciz. Susannah York adds: 'When Eloi first demonstrated to me in speech the Claudelian *verset* – Claudel's completely original form of free verse inspired by his reading of the Psalms – as a way in which a phrase or a thought could be spoken in a single breath, I suddenly understood how the verse could set the actor on a wonderful roller-coaster... how, indeed, the text was thereby *underpinned*. With very little change of wording I re-cast my version into an English equivalent and it stood us in marvellous stead'.

JONATHAN GRIFFIN:
A SELECT BIBLIOGRAPHY

POLITICS
Britain's Air Policy, Victor Gollancz, 1935
Glasshouses and Modern War, Chatto and Windus, 1938
Lost Liberty: The Ordeal of the Czechs (with Joan Griffin),
  Chatto and Windus, 1939
Alternative to Rearmament, Macmillan, 1936

POETRY
The Hidden King (a verse trilogy), Secker & Warburg, 1955
The Rebirth of Pride , Secker & Warburg, 1957
The Oath and other poems, Giles Gordon, 1962
In Time of Crowding, Brookside Press, 1975
In this Transparent Forest, Green River Press, 1977
Outsing the Howling, Permanent Press, 1979
The Fact of Music, The Menard Press, 1980
Commonsense of the Senses., The Menard Press, 1983
Collected Poems (Vols 1 & 2), National Poetry
  Foundation, Maine, 1989 & 1990

POETRY TRANSLATIONS
The Journals of Pierre Menard no.4 (Griffin issue),
  October 1969
Von Kleist: *The Prince of Homburg*, Plays of the Year,
  Elek 1969 (now available from Menard)
Fernando Pessoa, I–IV, Carcanet 1971
Fernando Pessoa: *Selected Poems*, Penguin Books, 1974
  (2nd expanded edn. 1982)
René Char: Poems (trs. JG or M-A Caws), Princeton
  University Press, 1976
Camoens: *Gentle Spirit*, The Menard Press, 1976
Jorge de Sena: *Sobra Esta Praia*, Inklings (Santa Barbara),
  1979
Jean Mambrino: *The Inner Gold*, The Menard Press, 1979
Jean Mambrino: *Glade*, Enitharmon Press, 1986
Rimbaud: *Complete Poems in Verse and Prose*
  (unpublished)

OTHER TRANSLATIONS
Montherlant (8 plays), de Gaulle, Giono, Kazantzakis,
Gary, Rostand, Huyghe, Lilar, Vallier, Barrault, Bresson

101

CONTRIBUTORS

Rachel Blau DuPlessis: poet and university professor (USA)
Keith Bosley: poet and translator
Tom Courtenay: actor
Jonathan Delamont: poet and literary critic
Christopher Fry: playwright
The Revd. John Gilling: former parish priest of St. Mary's
      Bourne St.
Giles Gordon: novelist, literary agent and obituarist
John Greenhalgh: lay administrator of St. Mary's Bourne St.
Ronald Harwood: playwright, actor and President of PEN
Peter Hiley: director of Lawrence Olivier Productions Ltd.
Roland Hill: historian and London correspondent of leading con-
      tinental newspapers
The Revd. Dr. Brian Horne: theologian and university lecturer
Bernard and Jane Horsfall: actor and actress/writer
Peter Hoy/René Char: university lecturer/poet
The Revd. Frederick Jackson SSC: parish priest
Ivan Jelinek: poet and broadcaster (Prague and London)
Louis and Annette Kaufman: violinist and pianist (USA)
Sir John Lawrence: author and diplomat
Karin Lessing: poet (USA and France)
Eugenio Lisboa: poet and diplomat (Lisbon and London)
Helder Macedo: poet and university professor (Lisbon and London)
Jeremy Noble: musicologist and music critic (Buffalo and London)
Paul Oppenheimer: poet and university professor (New York)
P.K. Paige: poet and painter (Canada)
David Pinner: playwright, novelist and poet
Lawrence Pitkethly: poet and film producer (USA)
Neville Price: borough librarian
Kathleen Raine: poet, scholar and editor of *Temenos*
Carl Rakosi: poet (USA)
Manuel Rosenthal: conductor and composer (France)
Dee September: poet (Canada)
Sebastian Shaw and Joan Ingpen-Shaw: actor and opera planner
Matthew Sweeney: poet
Frank Thornton: actor
Judith Thurman: biographer (USA)
Daniel Weissbort: poet, translator and editor of *Modern Poetry
      in Translation* (London & USA)
Susannah York: actress and author
Julia Farrer: painter and art college lecturer
Anthony Rudolf: writer, translator and publisher

MENARD/KING'S TITLES FOR 1991/1992

Mensagem by Fernando Pessoa
translated by Jonathan Griffin with an introduction
by Helder Macedo

*I'm Not Even a Grown-up: The Diary of
Jerzy Feliks Urman*
edited and introduced by Anthony Rudolf

Red Knight: Serbian Women's Songs
edited and translated by Daniel Weissbort and Tomislav
Longinovic with a preface by
Charles Simic and illustrations by Audrey Jones

Quatre Quatuors
Eliot's Four Quartets translated by Claude Vigée, with
an essay by Gabriel Josipovici and an unpublished
letter by Eliot

A Necklace of Bees: poems by Osip Mandelstam
translated by Maria Enzensberger with a foreword
by Elaine Feinstein

Flow Tide: poems and prose by Claude Vigée
edited and translated by Anthony Rudolf

Engaging Images: the Practical Criticism of Art
by Merlin James